MAKING A MODERN CLASSIC

THE ARCHITECTURE OF THE PHILADELPHIA MUSEUM OF ART

MAKING A MODERN CLASSIC

THE ARCHITECTURE OF THE PHILADELPHIA MUSEUM OF ART

DAVID B. BROWNLEE

PREFACE BY
ROBERT VENTURI

COLOR PHOTOGRAPHY BY
GRAYDON WOOD

Editor: Sherry Babbitt
Designer and compositor: Ingrid Castro and Alex Castro, Castro/Arts, Baltimore
Production manager: Sandra M. Klimt
Printer: Amilcare Pizzi, S.P.A., Milan

Printed and bound in Italy

All newspapers cited herein were published in Philadelphia unless noted.

LIBRARY OF CONGRESS CATALOGING-IN-PUBLICATION DATA

Brownlee, David Bruce.
    Making a modern classic : the architecture of the Philadelphia
Museum of Art / David B. Brownlee ; preface by Robert Venturi ;
color photography by Graydon Wood.
        p.   cm.
    Includes index.
    ISBN 0-87633-112-6. — ISBN 0-87633-111-8 (pbk.)
    1. Philadelphia Museum of Art. 2. Classicism in architecture —
Pennsylvania — Philadelphia. 3. Philadelphia (Pa.) — Buildings,
structures, etc. 4. Trumbauer, Horace, 1869–1938 — Criticism and
interpretation. 5. Zantzinger, Borie, and Medary (Firm)   I. Title.
N685.B76 1997
708.148´11—dc21   97–7682
                                                     CIP

Dedicated to
Robert Montgomery Scott,
President of the Museum, 1982 to 1996,
in affectionate recognition of his devotion and service
to this building and the public it welcomes

CONTENTS

FOREWORD

Intended for the pleasure of any person interested in architecture and the history of museums, this book also aims to reach two important groups of readers: those many visitors to the Philadelphia Museum of Art who marvel at its vast, honey-colored building with profuse detail married to austere simplicity, and those many others who have only admired the museum from afar, or on their television screens as a backdrop for a parade or a civic ceremony, without ever passing through its doors. Our hope, of course, is to turn the latter into the former, and David B. Brownlee's lively and fact-filled text, coupled with Alex and Ingrid Castro's enticing design using a wealth of new photographs by Graydon Wood, should go a long way to encouraging conversion from remote viewer to visitor.

Professor Brownlee's scholarly interest in the museum's building and its context gave us both an exhibition and a fine catalogue in 1989: *Building the City Beautiful: The Benjamin Franklin Parkway and the Philadelphia Museum of Art*. We are delighted that he was prepared to take up his pen again to such eloquent effect, and we are very grateful to the distinguished architect Robert Venturi, who knows this building so well, for his thoughtful and celebratory preface. Sherry Babbitt has deftly deployed her talents as editor, and Sandra Klimt saw this book through the press with her customary zeal for perfection. The efforts of four researchers contributed to the story which unfolds herein, and we thank Carol Hagan, Jessica Jewell, Carrie La Porte, and Nancy Miller.

From the moment it opened in 1928, the museum's building has been the pride and joy (and occasional despair) of generations of staff and volunteers who enliven it, striving to keep it in good running order and to fill its galleries with treasures to look at and visitors to enjoy them. Many individuals were enthusiastically involved with this project: reading the manuscript, searching in the archives for just the right illustration, measuring the great

9

bronze rings on the exterior walls, bringing their collective memories and talents to bear on any task at hand. We thank, in particular, Terry Flemming Murphy, George Rehm, Joseph J. Rishel, Louise F. Rossmassler, James Sutton, Dean Walker, Ellen Weiss, Suzanne F. Wells, and Dreck Wilson for their help. It was a newcomer to our midst, Stuart Gerstein, the museum's director of wholesale and retail operations, whose enthusiasm for a book on the building spurred us on, and it was a veteran of twenty-seven years, George H. Marcus, head of publications, who brought the team together to produce a book of the quality appropriate to its subject.

It is the staff's collective pleasure, in turn, to dedicate this volume to Robert Montgomery Scott, trustee of the museum since 1965, president of its Board of Trustees from 1980 to 1982, and president and chief executive officer of the museum from 1982 through 1996, in affectionate recognition of his love for this great building and his outstanding leadership in our efforts to make it a more beautiful, more secure, and ever more welcoming place.

ANNE D'HARNONCOURT
The George D. Widener Director

10

PREFACE

As a child growing up in Philadelphia I loved architecture in general and the Philadelphia Museum of Art in particular—inside and out—as an institution and a building.

I am sure the immediate allure of the building lay in its color on the outside—ubiquitous and vivid—deriving from its polychromatic terra-cotta details and sculpture, and representing and symbolizing classical Greek architecture and mythology at a time when archaeologists had discovered Greek architecture didn't mean pure white, as in Greek Revival architecture of the preceding century, but, rather, rich multicolor. A more subtle allure derived from the golden aura emanating from this building's wall and column surfaces of self-cleaning Kasota stone. Then there were the dramatic varieties of its settings, perceived picturesquely from across the river or monumentally, atop its stylized acropolis, as the termination of an urban axial boulevard.

Inside, the medieval cloister of the Abbey of Saint-Genis-des-Fontaines thrilled this incipient architect the most. The gallery ceiling above it was a realistically lit trompe-l'oeil sky with fluffy clouds hovering over the courtyard—which also contained real geraniums in pots! The period rooms, unique to our museum at that time in their quantity and quality, made the effect of the art immediate. I loved and learned from these architectural places that I could enter, where architecture and furniture were juxtaposed in context in all their immediate detail—especially including that of a Louis XVI salon, a Georgian Powel house chamber, and a Pennsylvania German kitchen.

I continued to love and learn from the art of this institution as my range of interests grew to embrace painting, sculpture, and other media, Western and Eastern. And the architecture of the building has been continually inspiring and instructive: there are, for instance, those boldly blank facades of the two wings that face the parkway and effectively read from a distance—where the lack of detail and thereby the grand scale work eloquently within the urban context. As an architect evolving beyond the Modern tradition, I had to learn the significance of scale—of multiple scales in exterior architecture, where the grand-scale elements look good from a distance and to a crowd and the small-scale details look good from close up and to individuals. I came to understand that grand scale creates a perceptual whole, while small scale creates immediate delight, making this civic architecture both monumental and friendly.

Then there are the complex lessons of urban design. The museum on its plateau taught the validity of exceptions within an order. As a young architect I learned to love and admire the gridiron plan—that largely American urban phenomenon—with its tense and vivid juxtaposition of consistency in plan and variety in architecture.

The Philadelphia plan is perhaps the archetype. Established by William Penn it represents the essence of the American city, where urban quality and architectural hierarchy derive not from an individual building's special location but from its inherent nature—where civic structures sit cheek by jowl with their bigger commercial neighbors but express their relative importance through the quality of their scale and the significance of their symbolism.

By juxtaposing diverse architecture within a unified plan the American gridiron city accommodates both unity and diversity. We have no consistent height limitations imposed for buildings along a Champs Elysées. Buildings on a street can vary not only in height but also in size, material, function, and symbolism; theoretically our mayor's house could sit across the street from a deli. Our buildings derive their hierarchical standing not from their ordained position but from their inherent character: our urbanism is egalitarian as well as diverse.

And our gridiron cities are never complete—they are fragments of themselves. Because civic monuments don't terminate their axes, our streets extend metaphorically to infinity— open to an eternal frontier of endless opportunity. Viva the fragment city!

Most significant are the *exceptions:* Broad and Market streets, for instance, connote a degree of hierarchy through their exceptional widths and central locations. And some diagonal roads juxtaposed upon the local grid acknowledge regional dimensions, as in the avenues to Lancaster, Baltimore, and Frankford.

And our art museum terminates a diagonal Parisian boulevard we call the Benjamin Franklin Parkway and gains a unique grandeur from its unique location within the urban context. And this eloquent exception proves the rule, making our gridiron order more valid and more vivid.

ROBERT VENTURI

13

Plate 1. A seated griffin acroterion surveys the
Corinthian portico of the east entrance

Plate 2. Corinthian capital and entablature

Plate 3. Corinthian capital

Plate 4. Ionic capital

Plate 5. Crest antefixes and bicolored roof tiles

Plate 6. The northwest pavilion above the retaining wall

Plate 7. Restrained wall details beneath an active roofline, with a seated griffin acroterion at the northwest corner

Plate 8. Eaves antefixes on the central block

Plate 9. Acroterion ibexes with a standing griffin and *pegasoi* in
the distance

Plate 10. Acroterion *pegasoi*

Plate 11. Paul Jennewein's *Western Civilization* on the northeast pavilion, framed by the Corinthian columns of the east entrance

Plate 12. A standing griffin acroterion astride the Benjamin Franklin Parkway

THE "WONDERFUL GREEK GARAGE"

On the afternoon of March 26, 1928, one of the most distinctive museum buildings in the world was dedicated. Thirty-four years in the making, the Philadelphia Museum of Art at last opened its doors on the rocky summit of Fairmount, aligned with the grand axis of the only recently completed Benjamin Franklin Parkway (figs. 1-1, 1-2).[1] Elsewhere in the city, new skyscrapers in the flashy Art Deco style were raising their shoulders above the skyline, electricity generated by the huge new dam across the Susquehanna River at Conowingo, some sixty miles from Philadelphia, had just come on line, and the Broad Street Subway was nearing completion. In the nation, Prohibition was the law, but the economy was an intoxicated runaway, and wealthy American collectors were acquiring the art of an impoverished Europe in quantities that alarmed Europeans.

The new Philadelphia museum was a strongly massed building of tawny Minnesota dolomite, confidently affirming the place of the arts in this dynamic time. Its Greek architectural elements were freely composed from a mixture of the Doric, Ionic, and Corinthian orders, and much of the detail was realized in vivid, colored terra-cotta.

Inside, in the largest museum building ever erected at one time,[2] an innovative scheme for the display of art was planned, keyed to the wants of both an impatient public and demanding scholars. The topmost (second-floor) galleries were to be devoted to a grand chronological sweep of selected masterpieces, assembling together the painting, sculpture,

Figure 1-1. Enthroned at the end of the Benjamin Franklin Parkway, the Philadelphia Museum of Art gathers the parkway's other cultural institutions at its feet and wears the green mantle of Fairmount Park around its shoulders. The museum was designed by a team consisting of Horace Trumbauer and the firm of Zantzinger, Borie, and Medary. The architects accepted the commission in 1911, but the building was not ready for operation until 1928.

furniture, decorative arts, and even the architecture—the so-called period rooms—of each era. Here the museum-goer of the Jazz Age could explore without any risk of "museum fatigue." Complementing this grand array, a series of "study collections" were to be assembled on the first floor—organized by medium and comprising all of the remaining holdings of the museum. For those who wished to examine a particular aspect of art in depth, the museum would thus be able to offer an equally innovative but very different facility. Offices, the library, and a large education department were assigned to the ground floor.

The archaeologically based polychromy of the new museum was enthusiastically covered in the architectural press,[3] and the efficient planning invited notice by museum specialists.[4] But the general public were less concerned with such technical details; they were captivated by the overall effect of the striking design and its stunning site above the city. Like all the others who recorded the opening events (fig. 1-3), the *Philadelphia Inquirer* reporter raised his eyes above the construction debris and as yet unlandscaped grounds and waxed poetic about the building that he encountered atop Fairmount, "standing clear-cut, serene and imposing against the smoky canvas of the western sky."[5]

Figure 1-2 (*opposite*). On February 17, 1928, the new museum dominates the raw winter landscape of the parkway, while inside, workers were making final preparations for the opening.

Figure 1-3 (*above*). Guests arrive at the museum's west door for the opening ceremony on March 26, 1928. At left stands the new Fidelity Mutual Life Insurance Company building, designed by Zantzinger, Borie, and Medary.

Six hundred invited dignitaries gathered for the dedication ceremony, ascending the hill to the museum under cloudy skies on that early spring afternoon. Although the building was externally complete, once inside the visitors must have noticed that much work remained to be done. Only twenty second-floor galleries—occupying much less than one-quarter of the available display space—were finished, and none of the first-floor study collections were installed. The room in which the guests assembled, the large gallery at the head of the grand staircase that was designed to house temporary exhibitions, still lacked a ceiling, and its exposed roof frame was concealed by a canvas awning, brightly painted in a Greek pattern (fig. 1-4). Nor had the Ionic columns in the stair hall yet received their colorful terra-cotta capitals (figs. 1-5, 1-6, 3-47). The guests overlooked these temporary deficiencies, however, and offered congratulations. Eli Kirk Price, the lawyer and public-minded citizen who had crusaded tirelessly for the construction of the parkway and the museum, spoke in tribute to the others who had labored with him, and his own "fidelity, sanity and patience"[6] were generously and rightly praised by former United States Senator George Wharton Pepper.

Figure 1-4. The opening ceremony was conducted in the gallery for temporary exhibitions, now the Kienbusch Collection "armory." This photograph of March 21, 1928, shows Leon V. Solon's painted canvas masking the unfinished ceiling.

Figure 1-5 (*left*). The great stair in the east hall leads up to the temporary exhibition gallery, visible between the central columns, and to twenty completed galleries in the north wing. The terra-cotta capitals had not yet been mounted on the Ionic columns when the stair was photographed on April 2, 1928.

Figure 1-6 (*below*). Interior perspectives, including this view of the stair hall, were drawn as the building neared completion during the winter of 1927–28. The artist appears to have been Julian Abele, the distinguished African American architect employed by Horace Trumbauer.

Pepper went on to sketch the new building's significance for the city's artistic life and its hoped-for relationship to the wider artistic world. Lamenting that Philadelphia, while devoted to the arts, had for so long lacked a first-rate art museum, he observed, "'The city culturally, has been a family without a hearthstone.'" The new edifice might supply that want, becoming "'the fireside of the traditional Philadelphian culture,'" but Pepper also warned his fellow citizens that they must look beyond their comfortable surroundings. "'The completion of a great work like this,'" he proclaimed, "'marks the death of provincialism,'" and Pepper labeled the museum "'a temple erected to pure beauty in a community of diverse religions.'"[7]

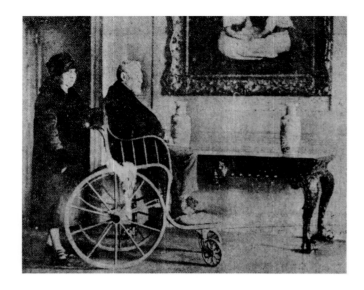

The thirty-nine-year-old director of Philadelphia's temple of beauty was the architectural historian Fiske Kimball. He spoke at the end of the opening ceremonies about the ingenious organizational plan that he had adopted for the museum's collections—and of the need to raise $1,850,000 to complete the building and implement his ideas.

While this was going on, five thousand somewhat more ordinary guests toured the building (fig. 1-7). They entered by way of the west lobby, a severe, almost undecorated space beneath the hall in which the dignitaries were gathered. Four columns of the simplest of the Greek orders, Doric, stood watch over the lobby from two lateral balconies (fig. 1-8). There is no report that first-day visitors used the intended general public entrance—a hauntingly beautiful vaulted tunnel that pierced the rock of Fairmount at the level of the surrounding streets and was connected upward to the museum by banks of elevators (figs. 1-9, 1-10). It was hoped that the city's subway system might someday be extended to connect with this subterranean entrance, and in anticipation a tile-lined station was built beneath it.

Figure 1-7 (*above*). Isaac Seligman and his daughter were the first visitors on the inaugural day of regular public operation, March 27, 1928. They are shown inspecting an Anglo-Irish eighteenth-century table and George Romney's *Portrait of Mr. Adye's Children* of 1789–90 from the George W. Elkins Collection.

Figure 1-8 (*right*). The severe simplicity of Greek Doric architecture defines the character of the west lobby, which still lacked a permanent ceiling at the time of the opening.

Figures 1-9, 1-10. Deep within the rocky mass of Fairmount, at street level, the designers provided a Piranesian tunnel lobby (below) for footsore museum visitors who wished to avoid the seventy-two-step climb up the hill. Sculptor Paul Jennewein designed bronze doors for the elevators that connected the tunnel lobby with the three levels of the museum above. The door panels, seen here in a photograph of February 3, 1928 (right), depict mythological beasts.

Figure 1-11 (*opposite*). The first galleries encountered by visitors contained the paintings of the renowned Philadelphia collector John G. Johnson, borrowed for the 1928 opening. Gallery 255 was dominated by Rogier van der Weyden's two-panel *Crucifixion, with the Virgin and Saint John the Evangelist Mourning,* of c. 1460–64 (left).

Figures 1-12, 1-13. The most elaborate gallery opened in 1928 was the rotunda (gallery 284) in the center of the north wing. Here museum director Fiske Kimball placed the bronze statue of George Washington, after Jean-Antoine Houdon, that had been given by John D. McIlhenny. The c. 1927 perspective of the elegantly coffer-domed rotunda below is believed to have been drawn by Julian Abele.

From the west lobby, the visitors ascended, first to the great stair in the east lobby and then to the top floor, where they could explore a small portion of the grand art historical survey that Kimball envisioned. The suite of twenty completed galleries, all in the building's north wing, was sufficient, however, to represent the director's thinking. One entered from the stair hall and passed through four large, axial galleries (galleries 250, 255, 258, 264) that were designed to offer no visual competition to the paintings they displayed (fig. 1-11). Decorated only by the restrained linear carving of their limestone doorframes, they were evenly lit from above frosted glass ceilings by banks of electric lamps, a system easily mistaken for skylights—of which the museum had none. For the opening, Kimball devoted two of these rooms chiefly to the John G. Johnson Collection of Renaissance paintings, loaned by special arrangement from the City of Philadelphia, to which it had been deeded at Johnson's death

Figures 1-14, 1-15. Adjoining the rotunda, two similar, barrel-vaulted rooms (galleries 283, 288) define the axis of the north wing. The two rooms were hung with American paintings for the opening and for many years afterward. In the 1934 photograph at right, gallery 283 displays James Abbott McNeill Whistler's *Arrangement in Black* of c. 1883 (left center) and John Singer Sargent's *Duchess of Sutherland* of 1904 (right center). The c. 1927 perspective of gallery 288 (below) seems to be by Julian Abele.

in 1917. Another gallery housed a borrowed sampling of nineteenth- and early twentieth-century French paintings.

At the "elbow" of the north wing, a cross-vaulted space (gallery 266) marked the turning and introduced the architecturally richer enfilade of five galleries that occupied the center line of this part of the building. Most impressive architecturally were the domed rotunda (gallery 284 [figs. 1-12, 1-13]) and the pair of barrel-vaulted galleries that adjoined it on either side (galleries 283, 288 [figs. 1-14, 1-15]). These more strongly ornamented classical rooms were intended to serve as the setting for American furniture, sculpture, and paintings—the latter largely borrowed for the opening from the Thomas B. Clarke Collection.

This enfilade of galleries also provided the spine upon which Fiske Kimball organized the first of his prized period rooms to be installed in the museum—four American and six British eighteenth-century interiors. His enthusiasm for collecting architecture was unusual, inspired in part by the successful but more limited use of the same strategy that had begun to be implemented by museums in New York and Detroit. In Philadelphia, the American rooms were placed to complement the adjacent galleries of American art (fig. 1-16), with the British rooms nearby to illustrate the relationship between British and American art in the colonial period. The British interiors also served the special function of displaying the Elkins and McFadden collections of British paintings, both of which had been recent gifts, promised to the museum with the stipulation that a new building be constructed to receive them (fig. 1-17). Kimball emphasized in all his public statements that the museum had on hand nearly a score of other period interiors, most of which had been recently purchased or placed on consignment. These included Italian Renaissance and French Baroque, Rococo, and Neoclassical rooms; a Gothic chapel; a Romanesque cloister and church facade; fragments from three Indian temples; and a Chinese palace hall. This fantastic array wanted only time and money

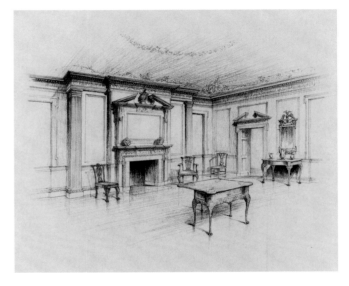

Figure 1-16 (*above*). Adjacent to the central suite of painting and sculpture galleries, Kimball installed four American period rooms, including the grand drawing room from the Powel House, built at 244 South Third Street in Philadelphia, c. 1763–72. Its rescue from a building slated for demolition helped to galvanize the movement to protect the city's colonial architecture. In the end, the Powel House was saved and equipped with a replica of this room, drawn here, most likely by Julian Abele, in a perspective of c. 1927.

Figure 1-17 (*left*). This oak drawing room was one of three interiors from Sutton Scarsdale, Derbyshire, England (1724), that visitors could compare to the adjacent American rooms. On February 3, 1928, English paintings from the John Howard McFadden Collection, including George Romney's *Portrait of Lady Grantham* of 1780–81 (left), awaited hanging.

Figure 1-18 (*right*). The underlying geometry of the museum is very simple, contrasting sharply with the tumbling cascades on either side of the monumental front stairs in this c. 1928 photograph.

Figure 1-19 (*opposite*). The angular, classical profiles of the art museum join those of the century-old waterworks in counterpoint to the framing greenery of Fairmount Park in Sigurd Fischer's photograph of 1928.

to be installed in the same fashion, and that thought may have helped visitors forget that most of the paintings on display in the new building were borrowed for the occasion.

Upon emerging from the museum late that afternoon, the guests discovered that the clouds had parted and the sun was working its magic on the mustard-colored temple facades and emphasizing with shadows the simple geometries of the huge building (figs. 1-18, 1-19). A closer look revealed that the apparent simplicity of the design concealed a great treasury of enlivening detail. In emulation of the many curvatures that the ancient Greeks had introduced in their architecture—supposedly to correct for optical illusions—almost none of the museum's stonework was simply rectangular. As could be detected easily by sighting across the faces of the masonry, each of the eight temple porticoes bowed outward in plan, while the plainly detailed connecting facades were concave. Moreover, the foundations of the two

Figure 1-20. The upward curvature of the museum's foundations was believed to offset the optical illusion that makes massive buildings appear to sag under their own weight. More recent opinion holds that such curvature was not intended by the Greeks to be an invisible "correction," but a visible enlivenment of the stonework.

corner pavilions swelled upward at the middle (fig. 1-20). More difficult to observe was the slight inclination of the great columns toward each other in such a way that lines extended from their axes would meet at a point two and one-half miles above the earth.[8]

An abundance of polychromatic Greek ornament was also clearly visible, although installation of the sculpture planned for the pediments had not yet begun. Faithful to the evidence accumulated by classical archaeologists over the last century, the colorful terra-cotta detail was concentrated high above the ground: in the capitals, in the complex moldings of the entablature that they supported, and in the antefixes attached to the eaves. The colors, still intense today, included Chinese red, gold, Prussian blue, yellow-green, and white, and this vibrant palette was used to make even the smaller ornamental details distinguishable from afar.

The stiff foliage of the Corinthian capitals that adorned the two largest porticoes, facing east and west, was outlined in black and highlighted in color, with the back of each leaf gilded (pls. 1–3, 14, 16). The loose scrolling of the Ionic capitals for the building's other six temple fronts was accented with blue, green, red, and gold (pls. 4, 6, 11, 15). (Similar Ionic capitals would soon be installed on the columns of the great interior stair.) Even more vigorously colored were the varied moldings of the entablatures: red and blue egg-and-dart moldings, blue and white rope moldings, red and blue tongue moldings, and leafy palmette moldings in black, white, and gold (pls. 2, 8, 17–19). Alternating fronds of the palmette antefixes along the edge of the roof were red and blue, and lion's-head waterspouts poked their muzzles out among them (pp. 2–3, pls. 7, 8, 15, 17, 19). The coffered ceilings inside the porticoes were not forgotten by the colorist: their moldings were colored as elsewhere, and each coffer was marked by a golden sunburst (p. 13, pl. 16). Even the enormous, three-foot-square roof tiles received color. Upper surfaces of grayish blue were combined with dark blue edges to make the roof seem to darken as one approached the building and the tile edges all came into view (pl. 5).

The same enthusiasm for decorating the upper parts of the building was evident in the bronze ornaments. Most visible were the enormous acroteria in the shape of mythological beasts that surmounted the eight pediments. The Ionic side wings carried paired ibexes at the peaks of their pediments, with seated griffins (griffins sejant)—beasts compounded of eagle and lion parts that were later adopted as the emblem of the museum—at their lower corners (pls. 1, 6, 7, 9, 11, 15, 17). Although not installed in time for the opening ceremony, pairs of winged horses *(pegasoi)* would soon crown the bigger, Corinthian pediments, and standing griffins (griffins statant) would take their places at the corners (pls. 1, 9, 10, 12). Punctuating the upper walls of the building were twelve-inch bronze ring bolts, imagined by the architects as anchorages for festive decorations (p. 2, pls. 2, 6, 7, 15, 18, 19).

As the first museum visitors descended the great flight of steps from the courtyard toward the parkway, serenaded by plashing cascades on either side, dusk was falling over the city. Street lights, held aloft on elaborate cast-iron standards, winked on, even as City Hall and the city's other tall buildings reflected the last sunshine.

In the months ahead there would be criticism for the design of the new museum. Hostile observers would call attention to the paucity of important paintings in the collection, decry the lack of natural lighting, attack the forcing of period rooms into an alien environment, and mock the anachronistic Greek references of the museum's architecture.[9] But although Fiske Kimball felt these attacks keenly, the innovative institution and its distinctive building proved themselves robust enough to withstand the complaints. Two-thirds of a century later, their vigor has been proven time and again, and the somewhat eccentric grandeur of the great temple on Fairmount has earned it a place in the hearts of Philadelphia's visitors and citizens. In 1928 the modernist painter Henry McCarter derided the museum as "a wonderful Greek garage"; if he were to repeat that epithet today, most would interpret his intended slur as a witty compliment.[10]

1. The story of the art museum and the parkway is told in David B. Brownlee, *Building the City Beautiful: The Benjamin Franklin Parkway and the Philadelphia Museum of Art* (Philadelphia, 1989), pp. 13–70 (catalogue of an exhibition held at the Philadelphia Museum of Art, September 9–November 26, 1989).
2. Richard F. Bach, "A Philadelphian Acropolis: The New Building of the Pennsylvania Museum," *Bulletin of the Metropolitan Museum of Art,* vol. 23, no. 6 (June 1928), p. 160.
3. Leon V. Solon, "The Philadelphia Museum of Art, Fairmount Park, Philadelphia: A Revival of Polychrome Architecture and Sculpture," *The Architectural Record,* vol. 60, no. 2 (August 1926), pp. 96–111.
4. E.g., Bach, "Philadelphian Acropolis," pp. 164–66.
5. John M. McCullough, "Twenty-Year Effort Ends in Opening of Art Museum," *Inquirer,* March 27, 1928, p. 1.
6. Ibid., p. 7.
7. Ibid.
8. Bach, "Philadelphian Acropolis," p. 163.
9. "$25,000,000 Art Museum, Ugh! Fine Greek Garage," *Record,* November 16, 1928, pp. 1, 4; "Museum's Walls Expected to Peel by Art Director," *Record,* November 23, 1928, p. 3; "America's Urgent Need Is Now Fresh Architectural Ways," *Public Ledger,* April 20, 1930, Music and Art section, p. 6.
10. "Museum's Walls Expected to Peel," p. 3; George Roberts and Mary Roberts, *Triumph on Fairmount: Fiske Kimball and the Philadelphia Museum of Art* (Philadelphia, 1959), p. 96.

The Museum in 1928

SIGURD FISCHER was born in 1887 into a family of painters in Copenhagen. After studying architecture in Denmark, he moved to New York and launched a career as an architect and architectural photographer, recording the city's Art Deco skyscrapers and other landmark buildings of the 1920s and 1930s. Early in 1928, Fischer captured the classical calm and the innovative polychromy of the Philadelphia Museum of Art with a series of photographs that could not disguise the incompleteness of the building or the still ragged condition of its landscaping.

Plate 13. The courtyard paving and the ramping walkways on either side of the great steps await completion

Plate 14. Corner of the central Corinthian portico, before installation of its griffin acroterion

Plate 15. Corner of the northeast Ionic portico, with its seated griffin acroterion

Plate 16. Polychromatic ceiling of the Corinthian portico

Plate 17. Seated griffin acroterion on the northeast pavilion

Plate 18. Ring bolt, anta capital, and moldings on the main block of the museum

Plate 19. Corner pavilion antefixes, lion's-head spout, and entablature

Plate 20. A figure provides scale beside the base of a Corinthian column at the east entrance

Plate 21. City Hall tower seen in the wintry distance from the east portico

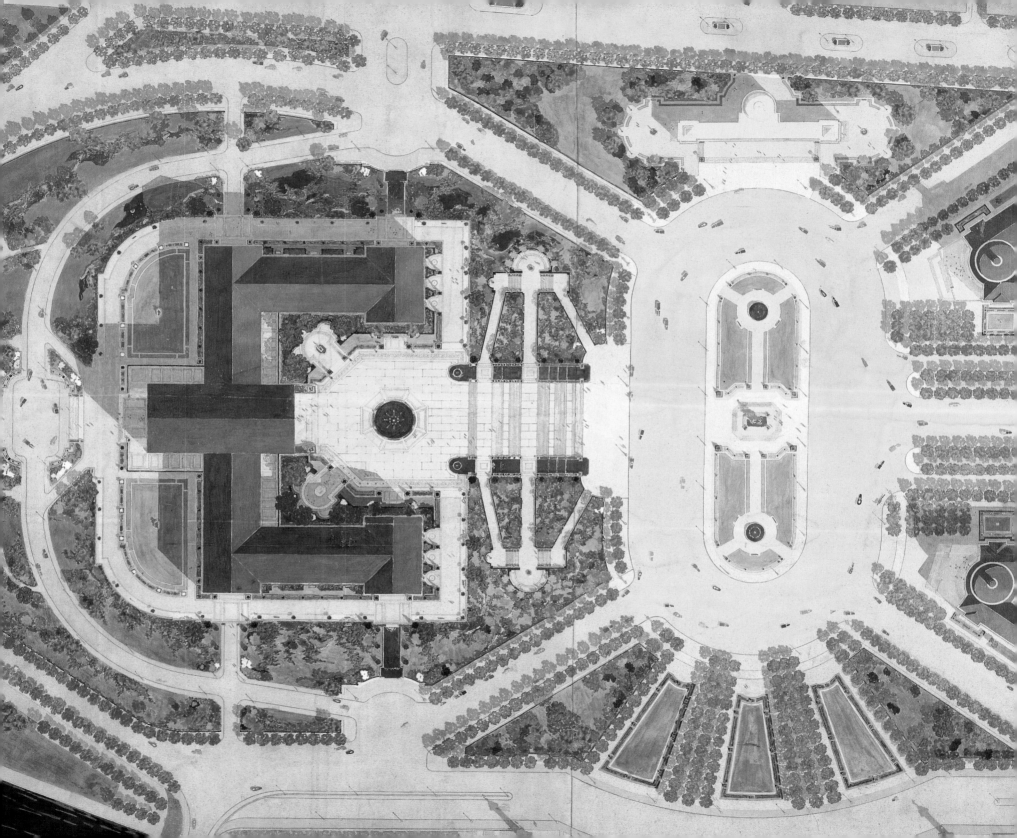

MANY ARCHITECTS, ONE BUILDING

When the Philadelphia Museum of Art welcomed the public to its new home on Fairmount in March 1928, it had been almost thirty-four years to the day since Peter A. B. Widener, the great Philadelphia art collector, had persuaded the Fairmount Park Commission to construct a new building. The museum's confident design concealed the fact that its history, like that of the institution for which it was created, was long and complex (fig. 2-1).[1]

Widener had made his fortune by assembling a monopoly of Philadelphia's streetcars and by developing real estate along the streetcar lines. He was prompted to begin the campaign for a new museum in 1894 by his dissatisfaction with the city's existing museum, then housed in Memorial Hall, erected in the center of enormous Fairmount Park as the art gallery for the 1876 Centennial Exhibition in Philadelphia (fig. 2-2). A number of circumstances suggested that the city could do better.

The inadequacy of the museum, to Widener's way of thinking, was inherent in both the institution and its physical setting. Founded in the wake of the Centennial fair, the Pennsylvania Museum (as it was called until 1938) ran a school of industrial and applied art, and, in conjunction with the school, it collected and displayed the kind of man- and machine-made artifacts that could serve as examples in the training of its students. Its model was the Victoria and Albert Museum in London, and at first it was scarcely an "art" museum at all, which was just as well, given its relatively remote location in the park and the unsuitability of its cavernous galleries for the display of paintings.

Figure 2-1 (*opposite*). The French garden designer and city planner Jacques Gréber was hired by the Fairmount Park Commission in 1917 to study the landscaping of the soon-to-open Benjamin Franklin Parkway. This detail from one of the gigantic watercolor plans produced in his Paris office in 1919 shows the art museum essentially as it was built over the next nine years.

Figure 2-2 (*above*). Hermann J. Schwarzmann (1846–1891) designed Memorial Hall as the art gallery of the Centennial Exhibition of 1876. After the fair, it served as the first home of the Philadelphia Museum of Art.

Figure 2-3. James H. Windrim, as Philadelphia's director of public works, prepared this proposal for the Benjamin Franklin Parkway in 1892. The bird's-eye perspective is from City Hall tower, with the Pennsylvania Railroad's Broad Street Station at the left and the Fairmount reservoir, the future site of the museum, in the distance.

The situation began to change in 1893, when the city received the bequest of Mrs. W. P. Wilstach, widow of a Philadelphia leather manufacturer, consisting of a not inconsiderable painting collection and an endowment of more than $500,000 to acquire more works of art. Here was the beginning of an opportunity, and the Fairmount Park Commission, to whom the city entrusted both the paintings and the money, immediately launched a purchasing campaign for the Pennsylvania Museum. The art purchases were guided in turn by Widener and John G. Johnson, the city's other great collector, and their personal collections were almost immediately added to the prospective acquisitions of the museum, in the public imagination at least. Compounding this happy circumstance was the rising enthusiasm in the city for cutting a new, diagonal boulevard outward through the congested center of William Penn's grid-plan city, laid out in 1682, to the edge of Fairmount Park. On April 12, 1892, the reform-minded mayor, Edwin S. Stuart, had signed legislation that created such a "parkway," although for the moment it existed only on paper (fig. 2-3). The parkway project afforded both a possible location for a new museum and a supportive atmosphere of civic improvement in which to build it.

Widener did not proceed indirectly. On March 10, 1894, he convinced his fellow members of the Fairmount Park Commission to ask the two City Councils (Philadelphia then had a bicameral legislature) for an appropriation to obtain a design for a new museum.[2] The money was approved, and in March 1895 a competition was announced for a site on scenic Lemon Hill, whose handsome Federal period house was to be sacrificed. The location had great advantages, however; it was far closer to center city than Memorial Hall and very close indeed to the terminus of the proposed roadway.

The competition brought forth sixty-seven designs from all across the nation and from several other countries. They were judged by a distinguished panel, consisting chiefly of nationally prominent architects. Local boosters were disappointed when the laurels were awarded to Henry Bacon (1866–1924), an out-of-towner, due in large measure to the failure of the contest to attract any of the bright young Philadelphia architects of the "Queen Anne" generation—notably Wilson Eyre, Jr., John Stewardson, Walter Cope, and Frank Miles Day. Judged objectively, however, the design submitted by Bacon set a high standard (fig. 2-4).

Bacon was then working as a junior designer in the office of the most prestigious architectural firm in the United States—McKim, Mead, and White of New York—and he would go on to later fame as the architect of the Lincoln Memorial in Washington, D.C. (1911–22). His partner for the competition, his young friend James Brite, was hospitalized with appen-

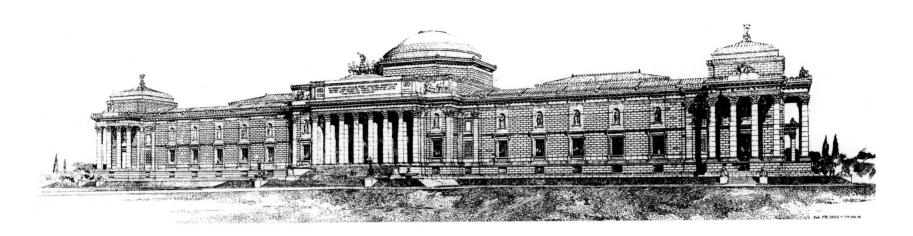

Figure 2-4. Henry Bacon, later the architect of the Lincoln Memorial, won the 1895 competition for the Philadelphia museum with this design.

dicitis in the midst of the work and seems to have contributed little.[3] Indeed the grave synthesis of antiquity and severe geometry that characterized the winning design borrowed many features from two of the big projects on which Bacon was then helping one of his employers, Charles McKim. The flattened, very Roman saucer dome, set back behind a stern, square-topped portico, resembled the Low Memorial Library at Columbia University in New York, designed the year before. The overall massing and the planning of the large building followed the precedents of McKim's Brooklyn Museum, designed during the same months that Bacon labored on his entry for Philadelphia.

The competition turned out to be a false start, however. Although the Fairmount Park Commission asked the winners about their terms and fees for overseeing the construction of a museum built according to their design, and although the voters approved $200,000 to begin the project in a loan referendum in 1897, no contract was ever signed.[4] A new mayor, Charles Warwick, had come into office, and he brought none of Stuart's enthusiasm for projects like the parkway and the new museum. Warwick was a stalwart of the fearsome Philadelphia Republican machine, whose usually uncontested stranglehold on the city earned Philadelphia muckraker Lincoln Steffens's epithet "corrupt and contented."[5] Although the machine bosses, with their close ties to local contractors, would ultimately be staunch advocates of these large construction projects, a strong demonstration of public support would

first be required. In the meantime, to prevent chaos in the real estate market, the on-paper parkway was removed from the city map.

Fortunately for the museum, the political bosses rather soon received the needed demonstration of interest. As the new century began, an impressive alliance of Philadelphia's leading citizens assembled to promote a local version of the growing "city beautiful" movement, the first important American contribution to modern city planning.[6] Inspired by the new boulevards and public buildings created for Paris by Emperor Napoleon III in the 1850s and 1860s, turn-of-the-century planners from all across the country promoted their own schemes for monumental roadways and commanding civic architecture. In Philadelphia, two organizations that had long supported other forms of city beautification, the Fairmount Park Art Association (founded in 1871 to place sculpture in the park) and the City Parks Association (founded in 1888 to promote the development of a metropolitan park system), took up this banner in 1900. The central goals of their crusade were the parkway and the museum. By 1902 their efforts had helped to spawn the Parkway Association, created with the sole purpose of boosting the project.

The Parkway Association brought together the richest and most powerful men in the city. John H. Converse (a partner in the Baldwin Locomotive Works) was its president, the brilliant lawyer and collector John G. Johnson was one of the vice-presidents, and its executive board included Alexander J. Cassatt (president of the Pennsylvania Railroad), Edward T. Stotesbury (a major partner in the Drexel and Morgan banking interests), and P.A.B. Widener. Mayor Samuel H. Ashridge, the machine's notorious "boodle mayor," was also among the founders. On June 12, 1902, they formally endorsed the creation of the new boulevard, with the construction of a new art museum identified as an integral part of the project.[7] More than a dozen editorials supporting the parkway appeared in Philadelphia newspapers over the next few weeks. With this invincible alliance of the city's financial, artistic, and political interests in the making, Mayor Ashridge signed legislation restoring the parkway to the map on March 28, 1903.

The hiatus had been fortunate, for in the meantime the city had announced its plan to stop pumping drinking water from the polluted Schuylkill River and to abandon the reservoir on the flat top of Fairmount (fig. 2-5). That hill, on the edge of Fairmount Park and directly on the axis of the proposed new avenue, offered a spectacular location for the museum, one-half mile nearer the center of the city than Lemon Hill, and magnificently visible from afar. Widener immediately shifted his attention to the reservoir site and vigorously pro-

Figure 2-5. Philadelphia on July 4, 1893, photographed from a balloon over Fairmount Park. The still water of the Fairmount reservoir is visible at the center, with the unfinished tower of City Hall above it.

moted its potential, but no decision about the museum had been made—and even the exact route of the boulevard was still being debated—when the city began to acquire land for the parkway in 1906.

The city demolished the first row houses in the mixed residential/manufacturing neighborhood that was to be traversed by the parkway on February 22, 1907, and less than two months later the project turned an important corner when Mayor John E. Reyburn took office. Destined to be Widener's ally, Reyburn had resigned from his fifth term in the United States House of Representatives to become mayor, and he returned to Philadelphia full of admiration for the celebrated "city beautiful" plan for Washington, D.C., that was being promoted by Senator James McMillan. (The "McMillan Plan" created the Mall that we know today: a broad expanse of grass lined by majestic museums and other public buildings.) Mayor Reyburn was also closely connected to Philadelphia's great contractor bosses, "Sunny Jim" McNichol and the Vare brothers, and so he was inclined to support construction projects. When Widener invited him to visit his palatial home soon after his inauguration, the mayor was thus in a tractable frame of mind, and Widener made the most of it. He showed the mayor a model of a museum, and he promised to build it on Fairmount at his own expense and fill it with his pictures, if the city only slightly shifted the parkway in order to insure its precise alignment with the building.[8] Reyburn was jubilant, and after touring the site on April 5, he told the newspapers that, except for the minor adjustment in the street plan, "'nothing stands between the city and Mr. Widener's splendid offer.'"[9]

The mayor's and Widener's project captured the public imagination, and the Fairmount Park Art Association promptly commissioned a study of the parkway–art museum combination. It sought the advice of four of the city's finest designers, bringing together a team of great talents and diverse views who would continue to be involved in the project until it was completed: Paul Cret, the partners Clarence Zantzinger and Charles Borie, and Horace Trumbauer.

Paul P. Cret (1876–1945) is the most celebrated of this group today—recognized as one of the leaders of the Beaux-Arts classicism that dominated American architecture and architectural education in the first third of the twentieth century. In 1907 the young French-born architect, himself a product of the Ecole des Beaux-Arts in Paris, had only been in Philadelphia for three and one-half years, having been brought to head the teaching of architecture at the University of Pennsylvania. But his influence was already being felt, as the Beaux-Arts movement converted one architecture school after another to the rationalist, problem-

Figure 2-6. Julian Abele played a key role in Horace Trumbauer's office. He is shown here with Trumbauer not long before the latter's death in 1938.

solving kind of classicism espoused by the Ecole.[10] Cret's already substantial prestige and his enormous charm earned him a position on the team of consultants for the new museum.

Clarence Zantzinger (1872–1954) was also a *diplômé* of the Ecole, and he and his partner Charles L. Borie, Jr. (1870–1943), a civil engineer by training, had already teamed with Cret on a project to beautify the banks of the Schuylkill River. In the future they would collaborate with the French architect on such important buildings as the Indianapolis Public Library (1914–18) and the Detroit Institute of Arts (1919–27). It was probably Borie's social connections that had help to land these young partners a place on the parkway-museum design panel.

Horace Trumbauer (1868–1938) was separated by a philosophical gulf from Cret and the Zantzinger-Borie partnership. He had trained in the old apprenticeship system that had prevailed before the universities had begun to found architectural schools, a movement that had only gained momentum in the 1890s. His architectural design work was more eclectic and less systematic than that respected by the Ecole and its American offshoots, and there was real antipathy among the others for his willingness to bend to the varying stylistic whims of his *nouveaux-riches* clients. But his office was large, with many talented designers, including Julian Abele (1881–1950), the first African American graduate in architecture from the University of Pennsylvania (fig. 2-6). Among the rich men for whom Trumbauer built castles, chateaux, and English country houses was P.A.B. Widener, who had commissioned the architect to design his huge neo-Palladian house, Lynnewood Hall, in suburban Elkins Park. It was also Trumbauer to whom Widener had apparently turned for the model of the museum that he showed to Mayor Reyburn in 1907, and these connections insured his place among the consultants.

The architects' report on the parkway, summarized visually by Paul Cret's bird's-eye view, combined all of the latest thinking about the project (fig. 2-7). The roadway was aligned to run squarely to the foot of Fairmount, and the site of the old reservoir was shown occupied by a domed museum, probably related to the design that Widener had shown the mayor. Reyburn now embraced the details of this proposal, and on November 25, 1908, with Borie at his side, he led a tour of the parkway route for city councilmen and for the leaders of other public institutions that he hoped to lure to sites along the boulevard. The party climbed to the top of Fairmount to experience the panoramic view that the new museum would enjoy. Afterwards, walking toward Reyburn's house at Nineteenth and Spring Garden streets for refreshments, the mayor pointed back toward the hilltop and proclaimed, "'That's where the City Museum will be!'" A councilman was overheard to say, "'Oh, let the old fool ramble on.

Figure 2-7. Paul P. Cret drew this bird's-eye perspective in 1907 to illustrate the parkway recommendations of a committee of architects working for the Fairmount Park Art Association. His collaborators—Horace Trumbauer, Clarence Zantzinger, and Charles L. Borie, Jr.—would be the designers of the Philadelphia Museum of Art.

It can't happen!'" But among those in the mayor's party was the lawyer Eli Kirk Price, president of the City Parks Association and vice-president of the Fairmount Park Commission, and he was impressed.[11] Price would join Reyburn and Widener in supporting the project, and it was his staunch support that would see it through to completion.

By 1909, after Price and Reyburn had lobbied long and hard, City Councils officially rerouted the parkway as shown in the Cret drawing, and the mayor was able to convince a large group of prominent bankers and businessmen to serve on his Comprehensive Plans Committee, designed to continue—with official support—the work of the Parkway Association. The new avenue was the centerpiece of the committee's deliberations, and it showed off its vision of that piece of the city's future at the Third Annual City Planning Conference, which brought delegates from more than one hundred cities to Philadelphia in May 1911. Prominent in the large model and in the set of drawings that depicted the project was the new art museum on Fairmount, conjecturally rendered for this occasion by William E. Groben (1883–1961), a talented young Ecole-trained architect in the Department of Public Works (figs. 2-8, 2-9). Philadelphia's energetic commitment to this "city beautiful" project earned widespread, admiring attention, countering the city's reputation for old-fashioned tastes and unchallenged corruption. Frederick Law Olmsted, Jr., like his father a celebrated landscape architect, praised Reyburn directly: "'Your city,' he said, 'is the farthest advanced in the country . . . in city planning.'"[12]

Figure 2-8 (*above*). In May 1911, Philadelphia exhibited its plan for the parkway in City Hall for those attending an international conference of city planners. Daniel H. Burnham's grandiose but unrealized Chicago Plan was on view in the room next door.

Figure 2-9 (*right*). William E. Groben drew this perspective of the art museum atop Fairmount for the 1911 city planning conference.

Figure 2-10. Two architectural firms were jointly commissioned to design the museum in June 1911, and they nearly immediately parted company. This severe, almost modern-looking elevation from late 1911 seems to have come from the office of Zantzinger, Borie, and Medary.

In 1911 Reyburn also secured the transfer of the reservoir site to the Fairmount Park Commission, and in June, hard on the heels of the big city planning convention, a special committee of the commission, chaired by Eli Kirk Price and with P.A.B. Widener as one of its members, asked a team of architects to make "a preliminary sketch for the art museum."[13] The team reassembled three of those who had worked on the 1907 report: Trumbauer, Widener's favorite, and the partners Zantzinger and Borie. (Zantzinger and Borie's new partner, Milton B. Medary, Jr. [1874–1929], was not officially appointed, but he did participate in the work that ensued.) Absent was Paul Cret, who may have foreseen that the wedding of such diverse architectural views would lead to conflict; in the end he made his own contribution to the architecture of the parkway with his design for the Rodin Museum (1926–29).[14]

The potential for conflict was almost immediately realized, because the two offices apparently chose to work independently, developing their own responses to the request for a "preliminary sketch." Both took the museum depicted in the 1907 bird's-eye view as a starting point (see fig. 2-7) and developed elaborations of that diminutive portrayal. In December 1911 the first fruits of this work could be seen. Zantzinger, Borie, and Medary had produced a very stern elevation for a building that, while classical in detail, drew most of its design energy from abstract geometry (fig. 2-10). Some echo of Bacon's winning entry of 1895 could be recognized in this as well (see fig. 2-4). The scheme from Trumbauer's office displayed a sharply contrasting philosophy (fig. 2-11). Its power resided in lush detailing and a very literal rendition of classical forms, most visible in the complete pedimented temple front at the center. The two designs were alike, however, in that neither was based on a deep analysis of the programmatic needs of the new museum. This was because the architects, who were working for the Fairmount Park Commission, had been given almost no instructions by the curatorial staff.

The committee charged with overseeing this design had stopped meeting by this time, leaving Price, perhaps with the advice of Widener, to direct the project. Not surprisingly, given Trumbauer's connections with Widener and Widener's still unfulfilled promise to pay for the museum, it was the drawing from the Trumbauer office that was selected for further development. The Trumbauer staff worked on this throughout the next ten months, and by September 1912 they had produced a strong and dignified design, resembling an enormous Palladian country house, with characteristic central portico, standing at the head of a prodigiously tall and wide stair that led up from the parkway (fig. 2-12).

Price presented this design to the Fairmount Park Commission on March 12, 1913, and with its approval he released the design to the press and forwarded it to the city's Art Jury, a new body whose review was required for all publicly funded architecture. The Art Jury

Figure 2-11. The Trumbauer office was partnered with Zantzinger, Borie, and Medary, and they produced a more literally historical design for the museum, with a Roman temple portico at its center, as seen in this perspective of December 26, 1911.

·PERSPECTIVE·

64

Figure 2-12. The Trumbauer version was selected for further development, and it was rendered in watercolor in this perspective of September 1912.

immediately referred the design for consideration to a subcommittee, chaired by Joseph Widener, P.A.B. Widener's son. Among its members were Eli Kirk Price and Paul Cret, and it appears that Cret, recognizing little of his friend Zantzinger's hand in the design, convinced the others to postpone their decision while he talked to the architects and tried to push them away from the emulation of historical precedents and toward a more original solution.[15]

In the meantime, other events were conspiring to lengthen this delay. In August 1913, using funds appropriated from the loan of 1897, the preparation of the site on Fairmount for the new building was begun, and the contractor soon discovered unexpected conditions. What had seemed to be a gentle slope on the southeast face of the hill, facing the parkway, was revealed by excavation to be "a nearly vertical cliff." This, more concretely than Cret's aesthetic concerns, would require the architects to make "a careful restudy of their plans."[16]

And there was no construction money, anyway, to be had from the new mayor, Rudolph Blankenburg, who was inaugurated in December 1911. Nicknamed the "Old Dutch Cleanser," Blankenburg was an even more wholehearted reformer than Stuart, and his mayoralty was Philadelphia's only full-scale experiment with Progressive politics. He was committed to

Figures 2-13, 2-14. The museum design was restudied in 1914, when preparation work on the site uncovered a steep cliff facing the city. Zantzinger, Borie, and Medary exploited that feature with a continuous facade that dropped down the face of the cliff to a public entrance at the level of the parkway.

unseating the corrupt contractor interests in city government. Wary of padded public works budgets, he appropriated no money for the still undesigned museum in 1912, and in 1913, with a design in hand but its approval deferred by the Art Jury, he was at first inclined to continue his moratorium on funding. Only a tumult of protest in the newspapers convinced him to try to divert a small amount of money from other projects. This arrangement depended, however, on the cooperation of the Republican-controlled City Councils, and they backed out of the deal at the last minute. At the same time the Councils were also rejecting the pleas of neighbors to close down the insalubrious pig yards in South Philadelphia, which were protected by the city's political bosses, giving the Democratic *Record* the opportunity to pin the Republicans adroitly with the slogan "We want hogs, not art."[17] But name-calling did not dissolve the impasse, and no appropriation for the building was forthcoming. The reformist mayor could only express the hope that "some public-spirited citizen may come forward"—an obvious reference to Widener's generous offer of six years earlier.[18] The collector did not come forward again, however, and when he died on November 6, 1915, there was still no approved final design for the museum. Widener's heirs made no commitment to keep his old promise to pay for the new building, although the possibility that his collection might still be given to the city tantalized Philadelphians for another generation.

Criticism, topographic discoveries, and lack of funds did afford the architects a chance to reconsider their work, and it appears that it was Zantzinger, Borie, and Medary, Cret's col-

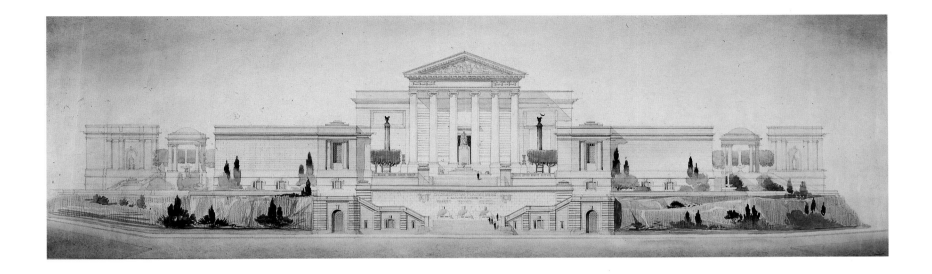

leagues, who undertook a restudy of the project at this time. They had to take into account Cret's distaste for the design submitted to the Art Jury and confront the problem (and opportunities) presented by the newly discovered Fairmount cliff. With no funding in the offing, they could proceed almost at leisure.

Throughout 1914, Zantzinger, Borie, and Medary experimented with the design, testing it with small study models. They came to favor a serene, simple design whose clear, French-flavored geometry and straight-linteled classicism seem to have been devised to please Paul Cret (figs. 2-13, 2-14). The design also turned the Fairmount cliff into an asset, giving up the monumental stairway of the earlier proposals in favor of a tall facade that reached all the way down—in front of the cliff—to the level of the parkway. There, convenient to pedestrians, would be an entrance and elevator lobby, with two floors of exhibition space above—on the top of the hill.

Apparently aware of this promising work, Blankenburg at last included the museum in his budget, and the voters approved a loan of $800,000 in November 1914. What the mayor did not know was that Zantzinger, Borie, and Medary had not finished experimenting, and in the spring of 1915 they turned the museum over to one of the brightest young men in their office, William Pope Barney (1890–1970). Barney repaid them with an entirely new conception of the building that once again delayed the project (figs. 2-15, 2-16).

Figures 2-15, 2-16. During the spring of 1915, the museum design was again reconsidered, this time by William Pope Barney, a young architect with Zantzinger, Borie, and Medary. This elevation (above) and bird's-eye perspective (below) of May 1915 show a grouping of buildings around a central courtyard, a concept that was adapted well to both the site and the possibility that the museum would house several quasi-independent collections.

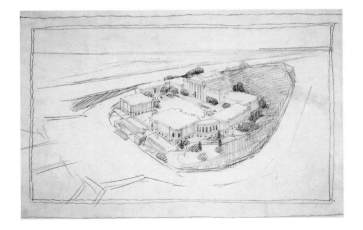

Graceful and unmannered, the design that Barney worked out celebrated the diversity of the museum's holdings (and the several private collections that it might attract) by assembling a number of quasi-independent buildings around a court of honor. The central block was stepped back from the cliff face to make use of the entire Fairmount hilltop, although elevators still dropped from the frontmost pavilions down to lobbies at street level.

This was a thought-provoking proposal, and it challenged Zantzinger, Borie, and Medary to reevaluate all they had done before. But they had little time to think before the Fairmount Park Commission issued an ultimatum in May 1915, pointing out that more than two years had elapsed since the architects had first submitted a design to the Art Jury and that, with funding now in hand, no further delay could be countenanced. Horace Trumbauer, who seems to have played no part in the recent project development, of course received a similar message. He had remained loyal to the 1913 design, compounding the problem of reaching a conclusion quickly.

It was Trumbauer, however, whose office worked out the solution. Among his designers was Howell Lewis Shay (1884–1975), a classmate of Barney's at the University of Pennsylvania (fig. 2-17). He would later make his reputation as Philadelphia's foremost skyscraper architect of the Roaring Twenties, but in 1915 it was his great diplomatic talent that was most needed. Shay has left a report of the frenzy of activity that followed the receipt of the letters from the Fairmount Park Commission that threatened to turn the work over to others. In it, he convincingly claims credit for working out a compromise design that took into account both the multibuilding Barney plan that had bewitched Zantzinger, Borie, and Medary and the Palladian design that Trumbauer had developed (figs. 2-18, 2-19). Shay's story begins with the warning from the Park Commission:

"Mr. Trumbauer showed me the letter. It said they had just three weeks to get the plans done—or they would turn the contract over to other architects.

"'I want you to handle this, Shay,' he said, 'or are you afraid of it?'

"I wasn't afraid. I had heard the three of them [Trumbauer, Zantzinger, and Borie] arguing many times. I knew why they hadn't been able to agree on a final design. Mr. Trumbauer wanted one monumental building to be at the end of the Parkway, like the one with the flat facade he had worked out before [see fig. 2-12]. But Mr. Zantzinger and Mr. Borie wanted the Fairmount 'Acropolis' to be more like the Acropolis at Athens, with several 'temples' around at random [see fig. 2-16].

Figure 2-17 (*above*). Under an ultimatum from the Fairmount Park Commission, the two architectural firms were forced to devise a compromise in 1915. They turned to Howell Lewis Shay, who worked for Horace Trumbauer, to develop what became the basis for the realized design.

Figures 2-18, 2-19 (*opposite*). Shay's design of June 1915, shown here in a first-floor plan (above) and a perspective (below), is the recognizable parent of the museum that was built, although ultimately the architects broadened the central portico, eliminated the ground-floor windows of the end pavilions, widened the outer wings, shortened the central block, and added a west entrance.

"I had to be sure they wanted me to handle it, too. But Zantzinger and Borie had seen my work, and knew of my awards [medals from the Society of Beaux-Arts Architects in 1912 and 1913]. 'You go ahead, Shay,' they said.

"'All right,' I said. 'Now, Mr. Zantzinger, you'd like to have it like the Acropolis at Athens. . . . Well, let's start with one big temple, right on the axis of this mile-long Parkway. I think that the tallest temple in the world is the Temple of Zeus, with columns 60 feet high—so let's make these columns 63 feet high, tallest in the world, a fitting terminus for the long vista.

"'Let's put one more temple on this side,' and I sketched it in, 'and another on this side, facing each other.' And Mr. Zantzinger and Mr. Borie were pleased, but Mr. Trumbauer had two more buildings than he wanted.

"Then I reminded them, 'Now we have to think about climate. Greece has very little rain, and mild temperatures. You can go between the temples on the Acropolis easily. But here we'd have rain and snow and you'd have to put on your galoshes. So why don't we connect these three temples with a series of galleries—exhibition galleries to house some of the art, big enough so full-scale rooms could be brought in—and connect these, forming a forecourt? That would make a beautiful approach from city hall down the Parkway.'"[19]

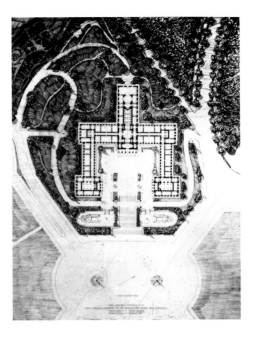

Figure 2-20. The central block of Shay's museum would have contained a prodigious single-run stairway, sheltered by the long barrel vault and lit by the axial skylight depicted in this perspective from the fall of 1915.

The disputing architects agreed to Shay's solution and set him up with a bottle of bourbon and a small office on Juniper Street. There, in ten days, he produced the design that was submitted to the Art Jury on June 21, 1915. Trumbauer later paid him a bonus of $350.

Despite the rhetoric of compromise, Shay borrowed only the idea of a court of honor from the design that Barney had prepared for Zantzinger, Borie, and Medary; otherwise, the design was far more like the work of Trumbauer. Ponderously if grandly historicist, it assembled three great temples facades—one Corinthian and two Ionic, just as finally constructed—around a central courtyard. Shay had taken the model of a group of temples clustered on an ancient acropolis quite literally. His plan was an enormous **E**, made rather ungainly by the backward slippage of its long central bar. Planned with grandiloquence but rather profligate in its use of space, much of the central block was occupied by a single-run ceremonial stair of staggering length (fig. 2-20), while many of the rather small exhibition galleries were strung along a wasteful system of single-loaded corridors. Shay, who would dabble in all of the exotic styles of Art Deco in the twenties, had already been seduced in 1915 by historicist detail and overall visual effect. The Art Jury liked it enough to approve the design "in principle."[20] Eli Kirk Price arranged for a big plaster model of Shay's design to be put on display just after Christmas in a special pavilion in City Hall courtyard (fig. 2-21). Despite a cold rain, holiday crowds of 7,500 came to see the show on the first two days of public admission, and the newspapers published the design with joyful thoroughness.[21]

P.A.B. Widener had died on November 6, 1915, less than two months before the model was unveiled, without his promise of funding ever being put to the test. But fortunately for the museum, if not for the cause of clean government, machine rule returned to City Hall in January 1916 with the inauguration of Mayor Thomas Smith. Twice indicted for election offenses, Smith took up where John Reyburn had left off, and it was under him that the parkway was pushed through to completion and that construction of the museum begun. Eli Kirk Price, the champion of both projects, guided the new mayor through the model exhibition on January 12, 1916. In the following year $1 million was made available for the new building and $9 million for the avenue leading to it.

The museum design was now undergoing its final preconstruction revisions, and even the model was subtly different from the original Shay drawings, with a wider, shorter central block fronted by a portico that had grown from six to eight columns wide. The Art Jury, which had still to give its final approval, continued to exhibit the caution with which it had greeted the original submission in 1913. Paul Cret, its chief architectural adviser, was now in

France, however, fighting for his native country, and so the Jury took the unusual step of retaining an outside committee of three renowned architects to offer advice. These were John Russell Pope, who would later design the National Gallery of Art in Washington, D.C. (1936–41); Burt L. Fenner, who, as a member of the office of McKim, Mead, and White, had played a large role in the firm's work for the Metropolitan Museum of Art in New York (1904–26) and the Minneapolis Institute of Arts (1911–15); and Arnold Brunner, who had worked with the famed planner and architect Daniel H. Burnham on the planning of Cleveland's vast "city beautiful" improvements.

Under their advisement, a rather slow review and revision of the design went forward. A great Corinthian portico was added to the heretofore blank west facade of the main block, which the committee recognized as the likely point of entry for automobile-borne visitors, whose existence had not been anticipated by earlier plans. The main block was further shortened, and its long, single stair replaced by one that broke at a landing from which flights departed to the right and left. The side wings were thickened and the proportions of the four

Figure 2-21. By December 1915, when this large plaster model (since lost) was exhibited in City Hall courtyard, the process of revising Shay's compromise design for the museum had begun.

corner pavilions made equal, permitting the more efficient planning of exhibition galleries along central corridors and the insertion of a two-story atrium in each corner. These were all welcome improvements, and in March 1917 the Art Jury granted its approval and the Fairmount Park Commission accepted the design.[22]

The architects now prepared a set of large-scale presentation drawings—including monumental perspectives by Julian Abele (figs. 2-22, 2-23)—and they also drafted construc-

Figures 2-22, 2-23 (*opposite*). Julian Abele's powerful perspective of 1917–18 (above) shows the sculptural friezes initially planned for the corner pavilions. A north perspective (below), apparently also by Abele, shows the tunnel entrance.

Figure 2-24 (*below*). Jacques Gréber portrayed the museum in several vivid drawings in 1917–18, including this view of the steps and cascades.

Figure 2-25. Gréber's 1917–18 perspective of the south corner of the museum shows one of two niches in the retaining wall that balanced the tunnel portals.

tion plans to guide contractors in bidding for the project. The Fairmount Park Commission itself directed Jacques Gréber (1882–1962), the French landscape architect and city planner whom it had hired to offer advice about the details of the rapidly advancing parkway, to add the approved museum design to his drawings. Gréber's energetic crayon perspectives and the enormous watercolors prepared by the assistants in his Paris office created an indelible impression of the great American building (figs. 2-1, 2-24–2-27). Bold in overall massing but lushly detailed, the museum was portrayed by Gréber and his associates with statue-filled pediments, enormous sculptural friezes stretching across the upper facades of the end pavilions, and a row of mighty Corinthian pilasters enlivening the long side elevations of the main block.

The final design was impressive, but it had not been achieved fast enough for John G. Johnson, the collector who had helped Widener launch the art museum project in the 1890s. His collection had long been assumed to be the future property of the museum, but on Feb-

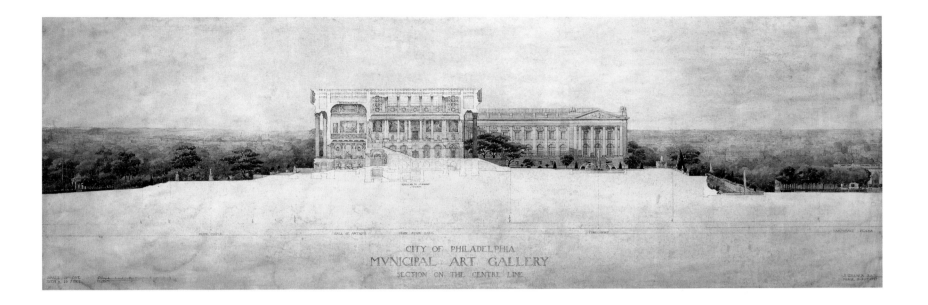

ruary 12, 1917, only a month before the design was at last approved, he revised his will to specify that while his paintings would be given to the city, they were to remain in his house at 510 South Broad Street.[23] In April, Johnson died, the second disappointed donor to take his dreams of the museum to the grave. In the same month the United States entered World War I, and the concomitant shortage of building materials kept even the energetic Mayor Smith from starting construction. Work on the parkway, largely a matter of demolition, was able to go ahead, however, and the boulevard was declared open on October 26, 1918. (In 1937 it was named for Benjamin Franklin.)

A lifting of restrictions on strategic materials preceded the Armistice of November 1918, and the mayor devoted his last year in office to a peacetime campaign on behalf of the museum. His enthusiasm won the cautious confidence of P.A.B. Widener's son and heir, Joseph Widener, who in December publicly promised his father's paintings to the city, provided that the city finally built the museum that his father had once offered to erect at his own expense.[24] The younger Widener also worked to have the Johnson Collection moved to a new building of its own on the parkway, where it might at least contribute to the aura of the bigger museum.[25]

Figure 2-26. Among the enormous watercolor drawings of the parkway and its proposed buildings that were produced by Gréber's staff in Paris is this section through the museum's west lobby and stair hall dated October 20, 1917.

75

Construction of the foundations for the museum on Fairmount began without ceremony on July 28, 1919, amid the usual charges of bid-rigging. In October it was learned that the notable collection of British painting assembled by P.A.B. Widener's late partner, William L. Elkins, would join Widener's art in the museum through the bequest of his son. Again there was a proviso: the building had to be ready for occupancy within five years. To this challenge Clarence Zantzinger replied with some bravado, "'Any building, within reason, can be finished in five years.'"[26] In fact, more than eight years would pass before even a fraction of the museum opened to the public, but during those long years some of the most familiar and admired elements were added to its design.

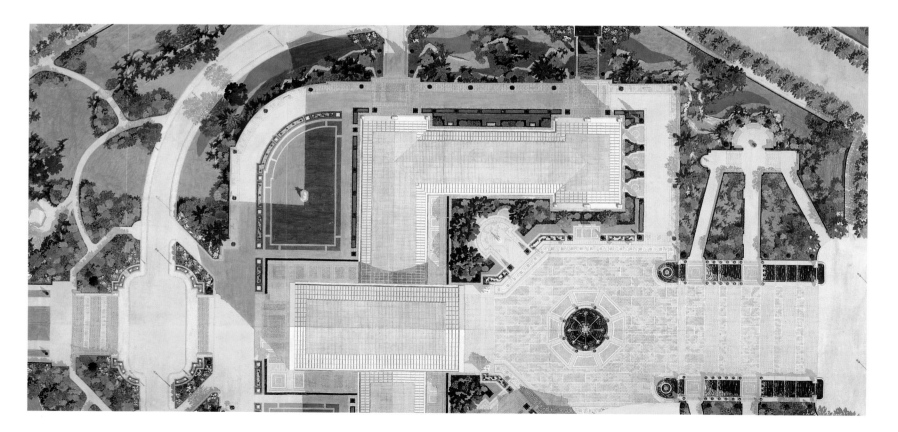

Figure 2-27. The elaborate gardens shown in this partial roof plan of the museum, prepared in Gréber's office in the fall of 1917, were never executed, and the skylights shown on the main block were eliminated after the architects decided to rely on artificial lighting.

1. This story is told in more detail in David B. Brownlee, *Building the City Beautiful: The Benjamin Franklin Parkway and the Philadelphia Museum of Art* (Philadelphia, 1989), pp. 39–70.

2. Fairmount Park Commission Minutes, vol. 9, pp. 257–58, March 10, 1894, City of Philadelphia, Department of Records, City Archives (hereinafter cited as City Archives of Philadelphia), 149.1.

3. Christopher A. Thomas, whose doctoral dissertation was devoted to Bacon ("The Lincoln Memorial and Its Architect, Henry Bacon [1866–1924]," Yale University, 1990), kindly shared his insights about Bacon and the work that was then underway in the office of McKim, Mead, and White.

4. Fairmount Park Commission, Committee on Memorial Hall Minutes, pp. 23–24, December 13, 1895, City Archives of Philadelphia, 149.22.

5. Lincoln Steffens, "Philadelphia: Corrupt and Contented," *McClure's Magazine,* vol. 21, no. 3 (July 1903), pp. 249–63.

6. Brownlee, *Building the City Beautiful*; W. H. Wilson, *The City Beautiful Movement* (Baltimore, 1989).

7. Albert Kelsey, ed. and comp., *The Proposed Parkway for Philadelphia: A Direct Thoroughfare from the Public Buildings to the Green Street Entrance of Fairmount Park* (Philadelphia, 1902), pp. 9, 22.

8. Brownlee, *Building the City Beautiful,* pp. 44–45.

9. "Widener Offers to Crown Parkway with Magnificent $2,000,000 Art Gallery," *Press,* April 7, 1907, pp. 1, 2.

10. The distinctions among the various forms of modern architectural classicism are explained in more detail in Brownlee, *Building the City Beautiful,* pp. 1–12.

11. Sarah Dickson Lowrie, "Price Papers" (TS), 1936, pt. 2, p. 54, Philadelphia Museum of Art Library.

12. "Mayor Is Chairman of City Plan Committee," *Public Ledger,* February 28, 1911, p. 9.

13. Fairmount Park Commission, Committee on the Art Museum Minutes, pp. 343–44, June 29, 1911, City Archives of Philadelphia, 149.18.

14. The Rodin Museum was created by Jules Mastbaum as a home for his collection of the sculpture of Auguste Rodin. Mastbaum died before the building was completed, and his estate was unable to establish the planned operating endowment. The city assigned responsibility for the operation of the building to the Philadelphia Museum of Art in 1939.

15. "Meeting of the Committee," March 26, 1913, Art Jury, file 81, City Archives of Philadelphia, 140.3.

16. "Art Museum," *Report of the Commissioners of Fairmount Park for the Year 1914* (1915), p. 9.

17. "Hogs, Not Art, Wanted," *Record,* October 4, 1913, p. 8.

18. "Expects Citizens to Aid in Building Art Museum," *Public Ledger,* September 25, 1913, p. 1.

19. Quoted in Doris Patterson, "The Invisible Man behind the Art Museum" (TS), [1973], Shay Papers, The Athenaeum of Philadelphia.

20. "Meeting of the Committee," June 24, 1915, Art Jury, file 81, City Archives of Philadelphia, 140.3.

21. "Structure Which Will Crown Parkway Shown in Miniature: Model Forecasts Actual Grandeur of Art Museum," *Inquirer,* December 29, 1925, pp. 1, 8; "Model of the Art Museum on View," *Public Ledger,* December 29, 1915, p. 9.

22. "Memorandum in Regard to Submission No. 81," March 13, 1917, Art Jury, file 81, City Archives of Philadelphia, 140.3; Fairmount Park Commission Minutes, vol. 12, p. 484, March 11, 1917, City Archives of Philadelphia, 149.1.

23. "Johnson Home and Art to City," *Public Ledger,* April 19, 1917, p. 4.

24. "Widener Tells Plan for Great Court of Honor," *Public Ledger,* December 6, 1918, pp. 1, 10.

25. For the Johnson gallery, see Brownlee, *Building the City Beautiful,* pp. 74–77.

26. "Elkins' Art May Be in City Gallery within Five Years," *Public Ledger,* November 1, 1919, p. 1.

LOCAL COLOR

The Philadelphia Museum of Art was constructed during the Roaring Twenties, and it was shaped by that era's tangled politics, its modernist art, and its debate about the public role of institutions like art museums. Fairmount's golden temple is a monument of the Jazz Age.

The actual construction of the building required almost a decade, and, like its planning, the work was often held hostage in the stylized combat between Philadelphia's ardent machine politicians and the rather mild reformers who occasionally managed to gain a foothold. As before, in the already long history of the building, the scruples of the reformers about spending tax money delayed completion, although they introduced the laudable principle of accountability into Philadelphia government.

The winter of 1919–20 saw the advancement of foundation work and the election and inauguration of Mayor J. Hampton Moore, who promised in his campaign to unseat "contractor rule" in the city. Commonsensically, the new mayor announced his unwillingness to support the pet plan hatched by Joseph Widener, which involved the city's commitment to build a second, smaller art museum on the parkway for the John G. Johnson Collection. Although this would have brought the Johnson paintings close to the big museum on Fairmount, while respecting the wishes of the donor to keep them in a home of their own, the mayor could see no reason to build two museums, or, as he put it, to "'scatter the pictures belonging to the city around in separate buildings to satisfy separate estates or individuals.'"[1]

Joseph Widener, loyal to the wishes of his father's friend Johnson, was chagrinned by this attitude, and on July 22, 1920, he quit the Art Jury, to which the Johnson Collection had

Figure 3-1. Inspired by the example of ancient Greek architecture, the museum was adorned with a vast program of colorful terra-cotta sculpture and architectural detail. The most striking element is Paul Jennewein's *Western Civilization,* fitted in the pediment of the northeast pavilion.

been entrusted. In an act of apparent pique, he also rescinded his offer to give his father's paintings to the city.[2] Eli Kirk Price immediately acted to effect a reconciliation, and Widener went on to serve the museum as a trustee and to campaign for the transfer of the Johnson Collection to its jurisdiction. But despite twenty years of pleading by the leaders of the Philadelphia museum, in 1942 the Widener art went to the new National Gallery of Art in Washington, D.C.

The uncertainty of the museum's claim to the Widener collection was partly offset by the news that John Howard McFadden, who died on February 16, 1921, had been more loyal, leaving his fine English paintings to the museum.[3] Like George W. Elkins, he imposed a deadline for the readiness of the new building, but McFadden's deadline was a more reasonable seven years.

Construction of the building proceeded under conditions transformed by the spirit of fiscal reform that had brought Mayor Moore to office. The Fairmount Park Commission's secretive handling of the slow-moving project, with the indefatigable Price trusted to oversee most details, was now the target of continuous criticism. In October 1921, a sleuthing reporter for the *Public Ledger* revealed that Price, Art Jury chairman John F. Lewis, and architect Charles Borie had refused to talk about the project, and Borie's partner Horace Trumbauer stirred a tempest when he told the newspaperman, "'Mr. Price . . . has instructed those under him not to say a word about the museum.'"[4] Price gradually learned how to work in this more skeptical environment, however, taking reporters and city officials on tours of the site and showing how, out of sight, two underground stories had been constructed, despite the slow delivery of concrete.

With foundations at last complete, the contract for the building's steel skeleton was awarded to the American Bridge Company on January 5, 1922. When this work also went slowly, Mayor Moore led another attack by questioners and doubters, demanding an accounting from the architects. Their report was made by Borie and Price at a special meeting of the Fairmount Park Commission on November 22, but it did nothing to allay concerns. Indeed, they delivered the shocking news that the funds on hand would suffice only for the construction of the steel skeleton, with $5.27 million more needed to put the building "under roof." Even then, having spent more than $8.5 million, the museum would be an unfinished shell, although Borie cheerfully predicted that it could be ready in two years—in time to meet the Elkins deadline.[5] Those who had visited the site must have found that hard to believe (fig. 3-2).

Figure 3-2. By January 26, 1923, the concrete foundations had been laid and the steel skeleton of the building was beginning to rise.

Supported by the press, Moore now demanded a full report on all contracts awarded to date, to which the leaders of the project responded with unguarded candor. Price riposted to one reporter, "'What does it matter what it costs? . . . What difference does it make? Who cares? All the people are interested in the Art Museum, not in what it cost. Look at it; the work speaks for itself.'" The same journalist received an equally ill-considered statement from Borie:

"We don't know now what it will cost to finish the building entirely. We never made such an estimate. How could we? How can anybody tell what it is going to cost? Why should we make such estimates? We are interested only in the designs and the plans, and that's all the public is interested in."[6]

On the eve of the January 1923 Park Commission meeting at which Price was to make his report on contracts to the mayor, the *Evening Public Ledger* broke the story that the very first contract, awarded in 1913 for site clearing, had not gone to the lowest bidder.[7] It was also remembered that the 1919 contract for foundation work had been questioned—and targeted by an unsuccessful taxpayer's lawsuit—and so it was to a hostile audience that Price presented his listing of the dates and amounts of the awarded contracts. With these data in hand, Mayor Moore demanded the creation of a small committee, chaired by himself, to probe these matters further, and while it reported no malfeasance (and thereby cleared Price's name), it mandated the public advertisement of all future bid invitations and the award of all future contracts to the lowest bidders.[8] With these safeguards in place, the Moore administration appropriated $7.5 million over the next two years.

In January 1924 Mayor W. Freeland Kendrick took office, returning the city to the more comfortable certainties of the Vare political machine. A contract for the superstructure stonework of the museum was at last awarded to George A. Fuller in March, and in April the architects quite blithely estimated that finishing the interior would raise the total cost of the project to $17 million.[9] Eli Kirk Price convinced the Fairmount Park Commission that the best way to schedule construction was to build the two outermost pavilions of the building first—and these were enclosed by the summer of 1925 (fig. 3-3). It escaped no one's notice that Price's stratagem would compel the city to pay for the missing central portion of the building, even if the political tide were to reverse again. There was, however, no way that even Price's cleverness and the more favorable disposition of city government could open

Figure 3-3. The exterior masonry of the corner pavilions was complete by June 30, 1925, when the contractors' photographer recorded this disconcerting image of the two unconnected elements.

the building in time to meet the five-year deadline in George Elkins's 1919 bequest, but his trustees generously accepted the exhibition of his paintings in an unfinished basement corridor in October 1924 as fulfillment of that requirement.

The seven-year deadline in McFadden's 1921 will was still within reach, and twenty of the upper-floor exhibition galleries were rushed to completion in the last months of 1927—Mayor Kendrick's last months in office. At its December meeting, the Fairmount Park Commission bade a fond farewell to the mayor and his chief ally, City Council President Charles Hall. The latter explained how the machine did its work:

When the Commission said that it would cost a certain amount to finish the exterior of this Art Museum, through the staunch support of his Honor, the Mayor, we made the appropriation. Some of my colleagues in Council, of course, did not approve of it. They have different interests and what appeals to one man particularly as a necessity does not appeal to another. I have been subject to some criticism for taking the advanced step that I have, and that criticism I am proud to receive.[10]

The building that opened in the first months of 1928 had cost about $12 million, and it was both incomplete and tinged by scandal. But the museum caught the public fancy almost immediately, with classical forms that were boldly and modernistically colored and an interior organization that reflected the thinking of the most forward-looking museum director in the United States.

The Philadelphia museum's eye-catching golden stonework and brilliant terra-cotta sculpture were created in the 1920s, when American architects were also building skyscrapers, schools, and stores that were designed to assert their presence in a world nearly saturated with the potent slogans of the first great national advertising campaigns and the new, electric imagery of radio and the movies. To make their buildings visible, architects experimented with exotic styles like Mayan and American Indian, splashed their buildings with color and geometric patterns, and invented Art Deco—the jazzy alternative modernism for those who loved ornament and had little patience with functionalist theories. Even skyscrapers that bore the imprint of Europe's more austere modernism, like the PSFS (Philadelphia Saving Fund Society) building (George Howe and William Lescaze, 1926–32), were inflected by American conditions, symbolized by the enormous rooftop electric sign that crowned that brilliant design.

Charles Borie was the member of the architectural team who bore the chief responsibility for the museum project during its long years of construction, and it was Borie who transformed the cool neoclassical design that had been unveiled to the public in 1915 (see fig. 2-21) into a bright-colored, modernistic temple. He took advantage of the long delay in starting work on the masonry carcass of the building to revise its design with a bold mixture of careful archaeology and advertising dazzle.

In 1921, with the signing of contracts for steel and stonework at last on the horizon, Borie worked rapidly to update the design, adding ornament and color wherever possible. In consultation with the museum's director, the Asian art scholar and archaeologist Langdon Warner, the architect worked out a plan to place sculpture in the three huge pediments above the building's courtyard porticoes and in the four pediments at the ends of its flanks. It was Warner who proposed the general program for the sculpture, showing "all ages and all countries bringing their gifts of art to America (or Philadelphia)." His favored sculptor, Paul Manship, was unavailable for this huge commission, and in Manship's place, Borie recommended Paul Jennewein (1890–1978) and John Gregory (1879–1958), to be employed in consultation with the ceramicist Leon V. Solon (1872–1957).[11]

This was a potent team. The English-born Gregory had studied at the Art Students League in New York and at the Ecole des Beaux-Arts in Paris. He had also won the coveted Rome Prize of the American Academy in Rome in 1912. After three years in Italy, where he drank deeply from the wellspring of classicism, he returned to New York and opened a studio.[12] Jennewein was born in Stuttgart and trained at the Art Students League. He too won the Rome Prize (in 1916), and in 1921 he had just returned from his own extended sojourn in Italy, prolonged by wartime volunteer service with the Red Cross.[13] The third member of the team, Leon Solon, had trained in ceramic design in his native England and had made a name for himself as a scholar and theorist of architectural polychromy. His inclusion shows that Borie had already concluded that the museum's sculpture was to be executed in colorful terra-cotta. Solon had caught Borie's attention with an article in the *Architectural Record* in which he argued that polychrome sculpture was inherently antinaturalistic and that it had to be considered a distinct art.[14] Solon adduced many examples from his study of archaic and

Figure 3-4. Greek architecture had been vividly painted. Benoît-Edouard Loviot (1848–1921), a French student in Rome, imagined the Parthenon decorated with these colors in 1879–81.

classical Greek sculpture to the discussion of polychromy, relying heavily on the work of German archaeologists from the 1880s onward, but he held that adopting modern materials—most notably glazed terra-cotta—would still require careful experimentation. That was what Borie offered at the Philadelphia museum.

The fact that Greek temples had borne brilliantly painted decoration had been known since the 1750s, and the early nineteenth century had seen ancient Greek color taken up as a banner issue by young French architects who were struggling to reinvent classicism in a more Romantic key.[15] But although the *pensionnaires* of the French Academy in Rome produced wonderful watercolor reconstructions of antique monuments (fig. 3-4), little nineteenth-century architecture had emulated ancient polychromy. The work on the Philadelphia museum therefore excited much built-up interest.

Borie's clients at first had little patience for his suggestions, but he played on Eli Kirk Price's youthful study of the classics and managed to win approval for a wide-ranging experiment with decorative color.[16] This was to be executed, under the guidance of Solon, in glazed terra-cotta in order to make it impervious to the smoky atmosphere of a modern city. In November 1921 the Fairmount Park Commission approved a contract with Jennewein to make plaster models for the proposed terra-cotta column capitals and entablature details.

The commission also assigned Jennewein responsibility for the conventional stone-carved decoration and the bronze sculptural ornament.[17] The first stone-carving Jennewein executed was on the museum's enormous retaining wall. This decorative work included four Greek mottoes, carved over the two large niches in the wall and above the two portals that were intended as public entrances (and that today serve as the loading dock and the entrance to the Wintersteen Student Center [fig. 3-5]). The Greek phrases were selected by Professor W. B. McDaniel of the University of Pennsylvania to celebrate the four primal elements: earth, water, air, and fire.[18]

Jennewein's most visible bronze work was the ibexes, *pegasoi*, and griffins that decorate the building's skyline as acroteria (pls. 1, 6, 7, 9–12, 15, 17), but he also designed the giant elevator doors on the inside (see fig. 1-10). Not all the metalwork was his, however; for example, the handsome brass and wrought iron window grills were executed by Tiffany Studios according to designs approved by the architects.

It was not only through sculpture that Borie intended to enliven the design of the museum. He also contrived to use the building to test another rediscovered truth about ancient architecture: that its surfaces had been subtly curved and inclined in order to correct—it was argued—the visual illusions that large buildings otherwise created. Borie secured the assistance of the leading expert on these "optical refinements," William Henry Goodyear of the Brooklyn Museum, who had summarized two decades of his own research and a century of previous scholarship in *Greek Refinements: Studies in Temperamental Architecture* (1912). Together Borie and Goodyear mapped out the incredibly complex instructions for the stone masons, who would be required to shape almost every piece of the museum's half-million cubic feet of masonry according to separate specifications. The effects were subtle, but an attentive visitor could notice a system of harmoniously overlapping curvatures. The foundations of the two wings facing the city curved up at the center, to compensate for the apparent tendency of a massive building to sag under its own weight (see fig. 1-20). The columned porticoes bulged slightly outward, to make them seem more robust, while the building's longer, plain facades curved inward to lessen the oppressive presence of their undecorated stonework. Finally, in order to appear as stable as they actually were, the huge columns were slightly inclined toward each other.

This alchemy in stonecutting and polychromy was complemented by Borie's decision to use colored building stone. After conducting tests in April 1921, he rejected pink Tennessee granite and resolved to clad the entire building in dusty yellow Minnesota dolomite, quarried from the Mankato and Kasota beds. Five shades of the stone were arranged with the lightest tones topmost, in order to increase the appearance of stability and strength.

To test the effects of curvature and polychromy, in 1922, as the steel skeleton was rising, the architects built a one-eighth-scale model of the building's northeast pavilion, which, like the other corner pavilions, was to be decorated with columns of the Ionic order (fig. 3-6). Solon recalled that when he and Borie first visited the model shop to inspect the unassembled wooden pieces, they

both experienced a pronounced sinking sensation due to curvatures on walls which seemed seriously distortious. The model was sent to Philadelphia for assembly in one of the old park buildings [a carousel shelter on the Schuylkill River below Fairmount]; when put together, these curves were only appreciable when sought, and a beauty and vitality imparted to the model which possessed a rare structural quality.[19]

Solon also experimented with color, using both the pavilion model and full-scale plaster mock-ups of the capitals and the other ornament that were to be cast in terra-cotta. The

Figure 3-5. The first part of the museum's extensive ornamental program to be completed was the sculpture on the retaining walls, which included Greek quotations. Homer's "Fire kindled by god," carved above the south entrance to the tunnel, evoked the horrific power of nature.

Figure 3-6. The museum architects resolved to enliven its masonry with curved surfaces and polychromy, and to test these effects, a one-eighth-scale model of the northeast pavilion was erected in 1922 inside an abandoned carousel building in Fairmount Park.

full-scale details were lifted fifty feet above the ground so that their effect might be properly judged. Solon reported that

in most cases ornamental scale which appeared quite satisfactory in the studio underwent radical change when hoisted to that height, as colors of a certain character maintained their actual area in effect, while others of another character appeared to shrink in area; this necessitated remodelling, recoloring, and a number of new calculations.[20]

In February 1924 the Fairmount Park Commission, satisfied by these experiments, approved the construction of a test section of cornice with the associated column capital, and in March it signed a masonry contract that committed it to the use of terra-cotta.[21] At the same time, accepting the plan for pedimental sculpture devised by Warner and Borie, it commissioned both Jennewein and Gregory to prepare one-third-scale pediment models, intended for the inner faces of the two wings that framed the museum forecourt.

Borie collaborated closely with Jennewein. The architect and the sculptor became friends, traveling together to Europe in the winter of 1924–25 to study polychromy, and while in Italy, where Jennewein returned to the American Academy as a visiting fellow, the two discussed and sharpened the somewhat muddy iconography of the two pediments. It was decided that Jennewein should represent Western contributions to art, while Gregory should depict the gifts of the East.[22] The yet unassigned central pediment was to show Art crowning all the nations of the earth. Unfortunately, while Jennewein immediately incorporated this new thinking in a small study model of the sculpture that he made in Rome, the clarification of the program was not communicated to Gregory in a timely fashion. Back in the United States, the two sculptors studied their pediments at one-eighth scale, which enabled them to test their effect on the architectural model (figs. 3-7, 3-8). Jennewein's *Western Civilization* was a loose conflation of early fifth-century B.C. Greek pediments, and Gregory, caught unaware by the change in program, had had insufficient time to disguise the fact that the models for his *Eastern Civilization* were equally Grecian. Resentful of Jennewein's close association with Borie, Gregory came to dislike his younger collaborator.

In the meantime, Jennewein's terra-cotta architectural ornament was being manufactured by the Atlantic Terra Cotta Company's plant in Perth Amboy, New Jersey. His study of the Corinthian capitals and entablature for the main block of the museum required the construction of a second model, showing that part of the building, in 1925 (fig. 3-9), and this was

Figure 3-7 (*opposite, above*). Paul Jennewein and John Gregory were commissioned to design polychromatic sculptural ensembles for the northeast and southeast porticoes of the courtyard. Jennewein's first, one-eighth-scale study for *Western Civilization*, with its central figure of Zeus (Jupiter), was mounted on the model of the northeast pavilion in 1925. Having already worked out the iconography with architect Charles Borie, Jennewein would need to make few revisions.

Figure 3-8 (*opposite, below*). Gregory's one-eighth-scale study for *Eastern Civilization*, also mounted on the architectural model in 1925, reflected his ignorance of the decisions made by Borie and Jennewein about the decorative program. Its incongruous central figure was the Greco-Roman goddess Aphrodite (Venus), flanked by winged Nikes (Victories), around whom gathered personifications of the arts. Only the vaguely orientalized dress of some figures—apparently a last-minute alteration—acknowledged the Asian theme that had been assigned him.

Figure 3-9 (*below*). A model of the larger, Corinthian portico, planned for the museum's central block, was built and linked to its Ionic partner in 1925, giving a foretaste of the grandeur of the courtyard.

88

Figure 3-10 (*opposite, above*). By April 1926, the sculptors had readied larger, one-third-scale models of their pedimental groups, and photographs of these were montaged with photographs of the nearly complete northeast pavilion. Seven years later Jennewein's finished *Western Civilization* would occupy the place where it was tested photographically.

Figure 3-11 (*opposite, below*). Gregory's one-third-scale model of *Eastern Civilization* was similarly tested by means of a photographic montage. By this point, the design he had presented a year earlier had been radically revised to reflect its Asian subject. His sculpture, however, was destined to remain a model.

Figure 3-12 (*left*). In 1927, models of the sculpture and full-scale replicas of the museum's terra-cotta ornament were shown at the annual exhibition of the Architectural League in New York.

Figure 3-13 (*below*). Jennewein won a medal of honor in 1927 from the Architectural League for his sculpture for the museum.

assembled with the other model in the old carousel pavilion to create the effect of the entire composition. In April 1926 the big-voluted Ionic capitals were mounted on the northeast pavilion, and since the sculptors had completed their one-third-scale models, photographs of these were montaged on photographs of the actual building and sent to the architects for review (figs. 3-10, 3-11). In August Solon published the one-third-scale models and a selection of photographs of the completed northeast pavilion,[23] and in February–March 1927 the two pediment models were exhibited at the forty-second annual exhibition of the Architectural League of New York, together with the breathtaking, full-scale section of the entablature and an Ionic capital (fig. 3-12). The striking polychromy—at once inventive and scientific— captured the spirit of the time, and Paul Jennewein received a medal of honor from the Architectural League (fig. 3-13).

By this time, enough of the actual museum's glowing masonry and multicolored decoration had become visible on Fairmount to attract attention, and newspaper columnist Mary

Like a giant having his butter cut for breakfast.

You can't scrape the gold off—it's burnt in!

Billy Penn should be proud of his Art Museum.

Dixon Thayer wrote a warm account of her visit to the museum construction site. She was delighted by the "tremendous pile of golden marble, crusted at the cornices with gold and red and blue," and she likened the mason's workshop, filled with huge blocks of yellow stone, to a giant's breakfast table, with butter sliced and ready for spreading on gargantuan slices of toast.[24] This whimsical conceit and others were illustrated with appealing cartoons (figs. 3-14a–c, 3-15).

In the rush to supply terra-cotta architectural decoration to the building in time for its opening in 1928, the fabrication of the pedimental sculpture was postponed. Even so, the building opened without the Ionic capitals of the main stair hall in place (see fig. 1-5). Solon continued to advise the museum on questions of polychrome decoration after the opening,

Figures 3-14a–c (*opposite, left*). On October 16, 1926, a newspaper cartoonist likened the blocks of yellow limestone, waiting for assembly, to a giant's butter pats and poked gentle fun at other aspects of the museum's architecture.

Figure 3-15 (*opposite, right*). By August 10, 1926, the great east portico was at last taking shape within the scaffolding and beneath the boom of a steam-powered crane.

Figure 3-16 (*left*). Left unfinished at the time of the opening, the ceiling of the great stair hall was given a test fitting with panels devised by Leon Solon in 1932. Solon derived many of the decorative motifs and the figural style from Greek black figure vase painting. The human depictions are a sculptor (left) and architect (right), suggesting that the program was intended to portray the various arts. Solon's work went no further, however, and there would be no permanent ceiling until the early 1960s.

and in 1932 large test panels that he had devised for the ceiling of the stair hall were hoisted into place (fig. 3-16). Because of Depression-era constraints, no permanent ceiling was installed in this area until the 1960s.

After a hiatus, fabrication of the already contracted Jennewein pediment went ahead once the building had opened. Unusually large kilns had to be constructed at the Perth Amboy plant of Atlantic Terra Cotta to bake the enormous statuary, and Solon adjusted the colors as they were realized for the first time in permanent glazes (figs. 3-17, 3-18). On October 9, 1932, the completed sculpture was unveiled at the factory, and then for ten weeks, between November 1932 and January 1933, a team of seemingly tiny workmen assembled the brightly colored colossi high up on the facade of the museum (fig. 3-19). Zeus, the central figure in

Figures 3-17, 3-18. In the fall of 1932, Jennewein's pedimental sculpture for the northeast pavilion was being fabricated by the Atlantic Terra Cotta Company in Perth Amboy, New Jersey. The infant Triptolemus (below) is as large as a mortal workman.

the composition, stood twelve feet tall and weighed almost a ton (fig. 3-24). The scaffolding was pulled away, revealing the work to full view, in March 1933 (figs. 3-1, 3-20).

Paul Jennewein's mighty ensemble of stiffly posed figures traced its historic pedigree to the pedimental statuary created for the great Greek temples of the first half of the fifth century, notably the Temple of Zeus at Olympia and the Temple of Aphaia on the island of Aegina. Indeed, the east pediment at Olympia centers on a standing Zeus, like the grouping in Philadelphia. The potent and deliberately antinaturalistic polychromy of Jennewein's figures was also based on what Solon judged to be ancient principles, although these were translated into modern materials with a resulting increase in stridency.[25]

Just as the figure types and their identities were ancient, they also told a story that was a pastiche of feats and foibles from classical mythology. As Jennewein explained it, the pediment depicts the influences that have shaped Western art, with the central, supreme Zeus (Jupiter) representing the "'creative force or the will of man,'" flanked by mythological figures who symbolize the two great defining themes of human art and civilization, sacred and profane love. These Jennewein called "'the physical and the spiritual elements in the nature of man.'"[26]

On the right of Zeus gather exemplars of sacred love, starting with Ceres (Demeter), goddess of agriculture, marriage, and other aspects of peaceful living. She holds the hand of Triptolemus, the child rescued from sacrifice by his mother so that he might teach mankind the value of life and work. Behind the youth branches the laurel tree into which the nymph Daphne was transformed to save her from profanation by the pursuing Apollo, and beside the tree sits Ariadne, who aided her lover Theseus's escape from the Labyrinth after he had

Figure 3-19. On November 16, 1932, workers were installing the Minotaur and the python on the right side of *Western Civilization*.

93

94

slain the human-devouring Minotaur (fig. 3-22). Theseus grapples with the Minotaur by her side, and in the far corner of the pediment the belly-crawling python represents the depths "'from which our spiritual natures are compelled to rise.'"

On the left side of the pediment are arrayed representations of profane love, defined by Jennewein as "'the physical, mechanical and scientific side of life.'" Aphrodite (Venus) stands next to the central Zeus, symbolizing love, beauty, and fruitfulness, with her son Eros (Cupid) at her side. Behind the little god of love is the lion into which Hippomenes was changed for defiling holy ground with his lust for Atalanta, the swift runner whom he had overtaken with the famous stratagem of three golden apples. Eros raises a hand in vain to warn the kneeling Adonis, beloved of Aphrodite, who is destined to disobey the goddess and hunt the boar that will slay him (fig. 3-23). Beyond Adonis sits Nous, the Greek personification of human reason, and in the corner, Eos (Aurora)—the dawn of the mind— turns from the owl, bird of the night.

John Gregory's pediment was never to be realized at full size, but the one-third-scale model fully embodied the intended program, devoted to the contributions of Eastern civilization to human wisdom (fig. 3-21). Lacking the variety of Western mythological sources employed by Jennewein, Gregory's interpretation was further hobbled by cultural stereotypes. He explained his rather lifeless composition as the reflection of his own, quite prejudiced perception of Asian culture, concluding that "'since the passage of time is a matter of no consideration to the Oriental mind, there exists none of the energy and animation so characteristic of Western civilization.'"

Like Jennewein, Gregory conceived the two halves of his composition as reflections of opposite tendencies in human nature, with material concerns to the right and spiritual values on the left. Balanced between them at the center stands the personification of India, understood by Gregory as "'the Source of Life, Philosophy, and Religion.'"

To the right of India, the world of material conquest and empire begins with the personification of Babylon, followed by Xerxes: "'King of Kings,' gazing sternly outward, typifying the lust of conquest." Beyond him sit the Sultan (fig. 3-25) and Scheherezade of *The Thousand and One Nights*, "'showing the magnificence of earthly love and luxury.'" In the pediment corner sits Confucius, the great moralist of the earthly life, with a Chinese dragon at his feet, emblemizing royalty.

To the left, India is flanked by the personification of Egypt, birthplace of religion, and beyond her stands Isaiah, the Old Testament prophet who foretold the coming of the

Figure 3-20 (*opposite, above*). Jennewein's *Western Civilization,* as installed in 1933.

Figure 3-21 (*opposite, below*). Gregory's one-third-scale model of *Eastern Civilization,* as now displayed in the museum's student center.

Figure 3-22 (*above*). Triptolemus, Ariadne, and Theseus, from Jennewein's *Western Civilization.*

Figure 3-23 (*below*). Adonis, Hippomenes as a lion, and Eros, from Jennewein's *Western Civilization.*

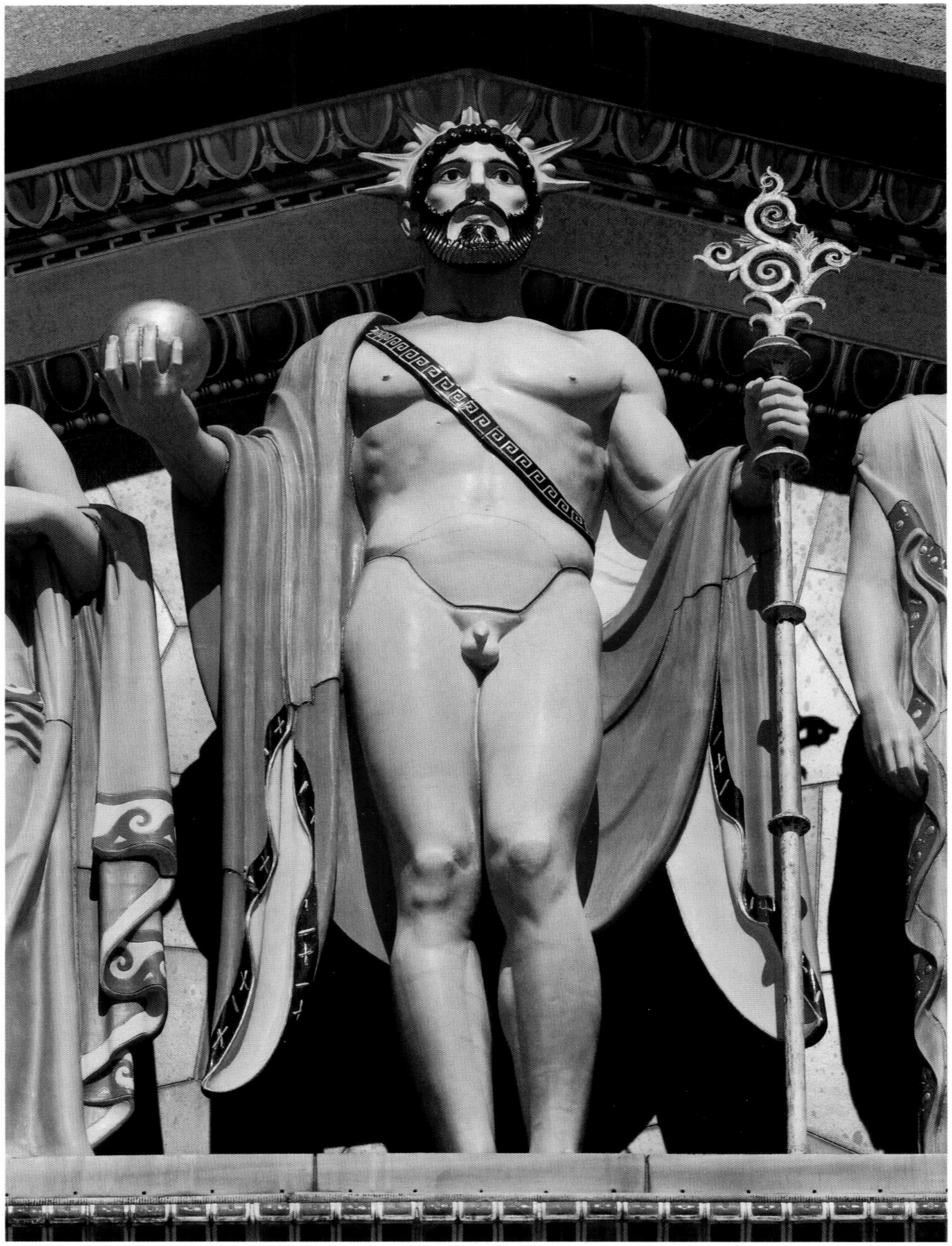

Figure 3-24. Zeus, from Jennewein's *Western Civilization*.

Messiah. Next in the array are the Rose of Sharon (fig. 3-26)and Solomon, "'representing the great romantic allegory, the Song of Songs, and setting forth a spiritual, not merely an earthly love.'" Beyond them reclines Buddha in contemplation, the spiritual foil of Confucius from the other side of the pediment. At his feet is the Foo dog, a Buddhist emblem.

The two pediments were generally well regarded by contemporaries, who were glad to believe that American learning, technical expertise, and sheer gumption could master and then surpass the achievements of ancient art. In truth, the work bore little serious comparison with Greek sculpture, and it suffered when such parallels were made. In 1933 Edward Alden Jewell, the critic for the *New York Times*, opined:

The color in Mr. Jennewein's pediment is charming, and it is to be hoped that similar polychromy may in time be employed for all of the now vacant triangles on the museum building. But it would scarcely do to compare, beyond this angle, the modern work and the best of that produced by the ancients. Many of the individual figures are nicely fashioned, yet there is so little unity in the group, so little true pediment rhythm, that these figures remain for the most part isolated and, in this predicament, sadly emphasizing the subterfuge that had perforce to be adopted in fitting them into the triangle.[27]

It was, most agreed, the simple novelty of the museum's polychromy that merited notice, but that notice was widespread and somewhat breathless. As Leon Solon, chief designer of the ornament, wrote, "Color is a terrific force when introduced into an architectural combination, and is capable of producing an effect upon the observer equalled only by the fascination which firearms possess for small boys."[28]

While the exterior of the Philadelphia museum was being dressed in pyrotechnic raiment, there was at first no matching vision for its interior arrangements. Langdon Warner served as museum director, with waning enthusiasm, until 1923, when he was succeeded by Samuel W. Woodhouse, Jr., M.D., designated only as acting director. Neither seized the opportunities that the new building offered, and neither articulated principles to guide its designers, who continued to work from the plans established in 1917. Charles Borie remembered that "'the architects were a bit handicapped in their work as we had but little idea as to the use to which the building would be put—after all the City owned damned little art!'"[29]

Figure 3-25. The Sultan, from Gregory's *Eastern Civilization.*

Figure 3-26. The Rose of Sharon, from Gregory's *Eastern Civilization.*

Figure 3-27. The most celebrated American architectural renderer of the twenties was Hugh Ferriss, and in 1925 he was commissioned to illustrate the art museum as it might appear when joined by other cultural institutions at the head of the parkway.

The president of the museum was John D. McIlhenny, an imaginative collector and a gifted, diplomatic institutional leader. He had shared with Eli Kirk Price the labor of pressing the city to complete the building, and it was he, seemingly alone, who saw the opportunity that lay ahead. In the fall of 1925, McIlhenny recruited a new director to Philadelphia, the architectural historian Fiske Kimball, who, almost at the last possible minute, defined the museum's mission and began to lay out the associated architectural requirements.[30] Only a few weeks after Kimball arrived, McIlhenny died of a heart attack, and Price succeeded him as president of the museum. Together, Kimball and Price put the new plans for the museum into action.

Created in 1876 as a repository for the study materials of its allied school of industrial arts and gradually transformed into the personal domain of a few aristocratic patrons and amateurs, the museum was to be reoriented toward the public and equipped with a building that ingeniously served a knowledge- and entertainment-hungry general population as well as a growing body of professional scholars. It was such a building, rising bright and inspiring above throngs of people gathered on the parkway, that was conjured in a dramatic perspective by the great architectural renderer Hugh Ferriss, drawn at about the time that Kimball arrived in town (fig. 3-27).

The new director brought impressive credentials to the work of building a museum: a professional degree in architecture from Harvard, a Ph.D. in art history from Michigan (where he wrote a thesis about Thomas Jefferson's Virginia State Capitol in Richmond), and a list of important publications on early American architecture. Kimball also boasted substantial administrative experience. He had been appointed in 1919 to head the new McIntire School of Fine Arts at the University of Virginia, moving in 1923 to New York University, where he created a studio and art history program in conjunction with the Metropolitan Museum of Art and the National Academy of Design. At both universities he had also served as campus architect. Museum expertise per se was another matter, however, and sensing his need to catch up, Kimball spent the summer of 1925 studying the major museums of Europe before taking up his position in Philadelphia in the fall. He came back with the seeds of a revolutionary scheme.

Kimball was particularly impressed by the Kaiser-Friedrich Museum in Berlin (today the Bode Museum), built in 1896–1904 by Ernst von Ihne. Its director, Wilhelm von Bode, had organized the display of the collection chronologically, with a relatively select, mixed group of paintings, sculpture, and furniture from the same period in each gallery.[31] This "cultural-historical" arrangement, Kimball recognized, offered a picture of human life and achievement that was far more appealing to the general public than the crowded galleries of most contemporary museums, with paintings organized by donor and the other arts grouped by material. He envisioned a hybrid museum, with Bode's system on the main floor and another floor of study collections, densely hung and arranged according to medium (ceramics, prints, textiles, metalwork, etc.). The latter would serve the scholar and the student, and would resemble the system already in use in the world's school-associated decorative arts museums, like the Pennsylvania Museum itself and the more famous Victoria and Albert Museum in London. Kimball explained, "In the museum of the future the aim will be to place the Kaiser-Friedrich Museum, extended to cover the whole history of art, above the Victoria and Albert."[32] His plan for the interiors of the vast, unfinished architectural carcass on Fair-

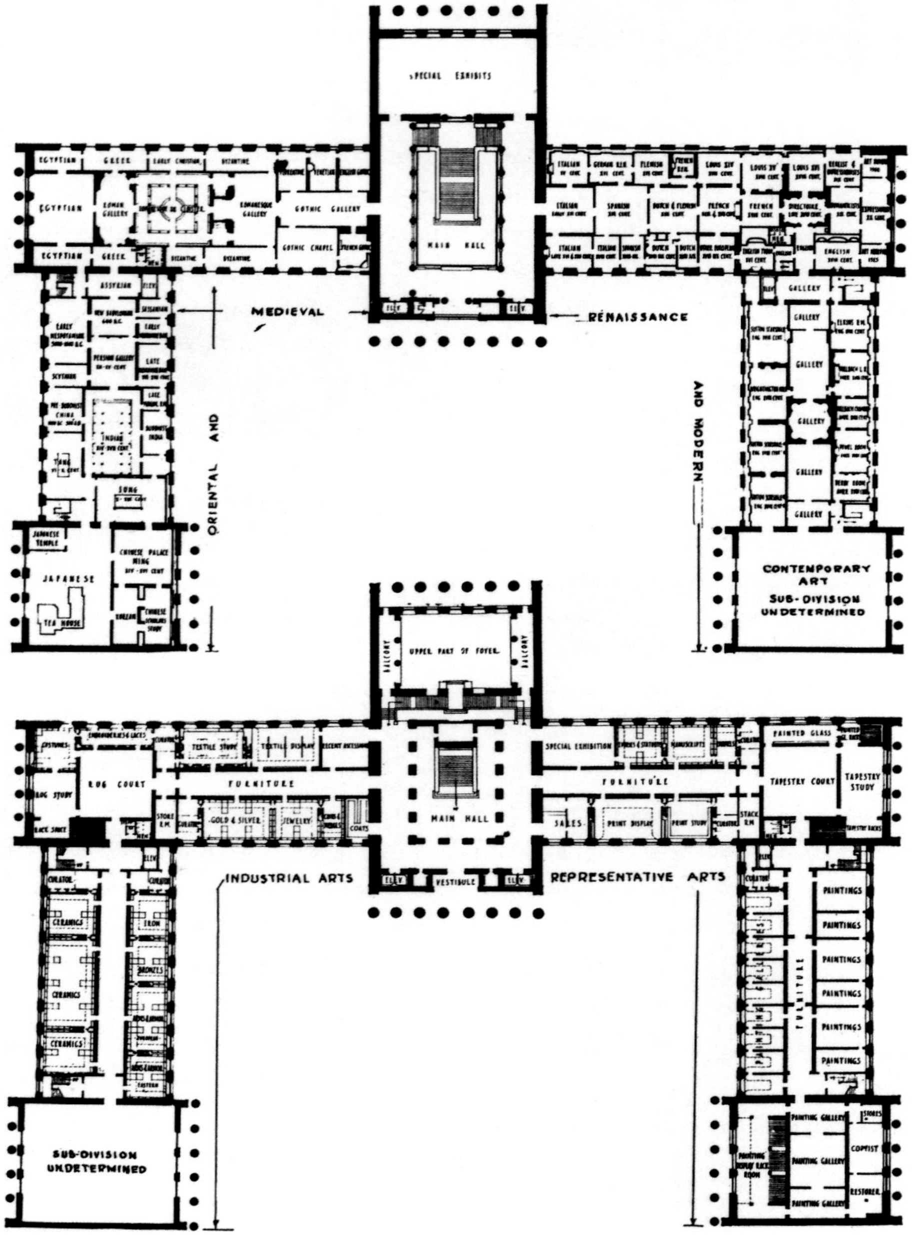

Figure 3-28. This second-floor plan of the museum (above), published in 1929, shows Kimball's grand sequence of period rooms and related galleries, and the first-floor plan (below) depicts the intended study collections.

mount followed that model exactly, with the second floor designed to serve the public and the first floor adapted for use by specialists (fig. 3-28).

Kimball fleshed out this organizational skeleton with a host of other important concepts, which he eagerly explained to the press in the year before the museum opened. Emulating the research of modern advertisers, his planning of public-oriented space was based on the scientific study of actual museum-goers. Edwards Robinson, a psychologist from Yale, helped the museum test the responses of its own visitors to the proposed arrangements, simulated in the old museum in Memorial Hall. The research confirmed that the new museum could be made immune to "the institutional ailment technically referred to as 'museum fatigue.'"[33]

The first ingredient of the antitoxin for "museum fatigue" was a highly selective display of the museum's treasures; as Kimball said, "The ordinary visitor wants to see the masterpieces; to find the finest things without tiresome search." These would be compounded in a special emulsion: arranged chronologically, as in the Kaiser-Friedrich Museum, so that "'by following only the "main street" of the museum, the visitor will retrace the great pageant of the evolution of European art from the time of Christ onward to the most vitally modern contemporary work, or, in Asia, from the austere beginnings in India and China to the last flowering of the delicate art of Japan.'"[34] The axial galleries that constituted this main street would mix painting and the other arts, and they would be flanked by authentic architectural interiors—"period rooms"—that would display the art of their times in even more authentic settings. The Philadelphia visitor would thus find none of the usual art museum's "wearisome succession of echoing galleries with bare walls and neutral backgrounds, and paintings, paintings, paintings, alone, without end."[35]

Period rooms were a relatively new innovation in American museum practice, and while the Philadelphia museum itself had acquired two such architectural ensembles before Kimball's arrival,[36] it was the example of the Metropolitan Museum's American section, reinstalled in 1924 with thirteen period rooms, that proved the attractiveness of the idea. Naturally, as an architectural historian, Kimball was predisposed to include architecture among the fine arts, and he turned his immediate attention to the acquisition of a suite of interiors for Philadelphia that would outstrip New York's. Between 1925 and 1931, twenty-five interiors were secured despite enormous obstacles—most notably the French enactment of a virtual ban on the export of architectural antiquities in 1927. Ten rooms—all American and English—were ready for the museum's opening in March 1928, by which time the plan

Figure 3-29. The glass ceilings in many galleries resemble sky-lights, but the light that comes through them is artificial. The original incandescent equipment has been replaced by the modern lamps shown here.

for the entire second-floor installation was fixed in Kimball's mind. Renaissance through eighteenth-century European and American rooms were to be arranged roughly chronologically in the north wing, with medieval Europe leading the way to Persia, India, China, and Japan to the south. (The absence of the ancient art of the West in the museum's collections stems from a long-standing agreement on the division of labor between the art museum and the University of Pennsylvania. Negotiated in 1929—when Kimball's curator of Eastern art, Horace H. F. Jayne, became director of the University Museum—and put into effect in 1932, this understanding assigned responsibility to the university for Mesopotamian, Egyptian, Roman, Greek, and pre-Columbian antiquity, along with the tribal arts of Oceania and Africa.)

The proper lighting of the collections was considered just as systematically as their arrangement, and in the end Kimball decided to reject sky lighting, although this had been embraced as the optimum solution by most nineteenth-century museum designers. Kimball concluded that the "glare of top-lighted galleries" was a contributor to "museum fatigue," and so he directed the architects to provide indirect electrical illumination, making the most of modern technology.[37] This would have the added benefit of allowing the museum to operate at night.

The impressive details of the lighting system were worked out by a team of General Electric engineers, led by Ward Harrison.[38] The largest and simplest galleries were given frosted glass ceilings, above which batteries of floodlights were aimed to illuminate the four walls evenly (fig. 3-29). The more architecturally ambitious galleries, located axially among the English and American period rooms, were lit through clerestory windows in their vaulted ceilings, behind each of which a 1,000-watt projector flooded the opposite wall while banks of 200-watt bulbs lit the windows to imitate the effect of daylight (figs. 3-30, 3-31). The greatest challenge was posed by the period rooms themselves, where it was impossible to supply sufficient illumination through the historic windows, making it necessary to insert lighting in the ceilings. A G.E. engineer described the daring solution:

In order to accommodate floodlight projectors to light the walls predominantly[,] the architects have, in effect, taken a sharp knife and cut through the ceiling about four feet from the wall all around. Then the inner edges of this incision are bent down about six inches leaving the central portion of the ceiling in a gracefully curved arch. This allows a band of stippled glass to be inserted, or a cove, if you will, inset into the ceiling behind which are mounted floodlights which sweep the walls.[39]

This architectural surgery escaped the notice of all but the most knowledgeable viewers, but, owing to its great difficulty, it was abandoned after the first group of period room installations (see fig. 1-17). Even they have now been retrofitted with more conventional indirect lighting.

The efficient ventilation of the museum's galleries was also carefully studied. Kimball approved a powerful forced-air system, with provisions for wintertime heating and humidification. Air conditioning, then in its infancy, was rejected as too costly.

Beneath the great second-floor galleries of Kimball's "main street" of art, the first floor was to be devoted to study collections, systematically organized by material and technique to facilitate the research of experts and promote the inspiration of students. Although the audience here was specialized, the same principle of public service applied, as Kimball analogized: "Like the special collections in a great public library, they [the study galleries] will have doors, closed, but opening at the lightest touch."[40]

Figures 3-30, 3-31. The original lamp units (above) were designed to be lowered into lamp boxes (below), which screened out distracting views from the galleries into the space above the ceiling.

Here, as almost everywhere, public education was the uniting theme of Kimball's planning. As he explained in 1928, no sector of the populace was to be neglected:

"To minister to the public . . ., museums have developed in the last two decades an actively and highly organized 'educational work.' Its different branches are directed not only to art students, but to students in the public and private schools, as well as the colleges and universities, to designers and craftsmen, buyers and salespeople, to teachers and prospective teachers, to parents, to clubs and to the unorganized public, including the casual visitor."[41]

Kimball studied the practices at other museums while devising the optimum layout for his education department—to be equipped with classrooms and a public library and located on the ground floor so that it could be open when the rest of the museum was closed. His dedication to these aspects of the museum's mission was rewarded by an extraordinary grant of $350,000 from the General Education Board, established by John D. Rockefeller in 1902. The award, requiring a match of $650,000 from other sources, was the first given by the board to a museum; it was announced only months before the building opened.[42]

A consummate showman, Kimball saw to it that the innovative features and the continuing financial needs of his project received maximum publicity during the many opening events, which extended through the first months of 1928. Even though no paintings had yet been hung in the galleries, the press preview on January 3 inspired Sarah D. Lowrie to gush in her *Public Ledger* column about her ascent toward the "grave and imposing portals" on Fairmount: "It gave me a feeling that mountains give you, that the sea gives you. If you were a Victorian you would call it—sublime."[43]

More than six hundred prospective donors to the Museum Fund toured the galleries (now filled with painting and furniture) in a glittering society opening on the evening of March 7. They were riveted by museum trustee Joseph Widener's impassioned plea for the permanent transfer to the museum of the Johnson Collection, some of which had been borrowed for the inaugural events. He also commanded them to stand for a few minutes of silent tribute to William Elkins, George Elkins, and John McFadden, who had given their paintings to the museum. This moving ceremony kept the issue of the Johnson Collection alive, and it gave Kimball a splendid opportunity to explain the need to raise $1,850,000 with which to continue the installation of the galleries and realize his vision of a modern education department.[44]

Figure 3-32. The chorus of *Houseboat on the Styx*, then playing at a Philadelphia theater, was attracted to the museum's portico for an early celebration of May Day on April 30, 1929.

Fund raising was advanced even more overtly at the next opening on March 13, which brought some one thousand guests to hear the French ambassador, Paul Claudel, speak eloquently of the "wordless language" of art. The audience also listened to Kimball's appeal for the funds needed to keep that language alive. Each guest was given two cards—one to record a personal gift to the fund and another with which they were expected to secure the pledge of a friend.[45]

After so much advance publicity, the official opening on March 26, with speeches by the mayor and other dignitaries, threatened to be anticlimactic, but the event managed to raise public appreciation of the achievement to a yet higher level.[46] The newspapers, even the most Republican-inclined of which had criticized the project's seemingly ungovernable expense, now relented. The *Inquirer* positively burbled: "The Museum has cost money, and a lot of it, but who shall say that every dollar expended on it is not more than justified?" And the *Bulletin* editorialized a paean to "the Temple, where Art is enthroned, glorified and to be worshiped."[47]

Although very little of the museum was complete, the public thronged in. The symbolically important first member of the public to enter the building on March 27 was Isaac Seligman, whose wheelchair was pushed through the galleries by his daughter (see fig. 1-7). He was followed by nearly ten thousand visitors on the first two public days and by nearly one million in the first year. When the latter figure was combined with the annual attendance at Memorial Hall—where certain collections were still displayed—Philadelphia's museumgoers numbered just sixty-seven thousand fewer than the visitors to the much larger Metropolitan Museum of Art in New York.[48] With characteristic scientific zeal, Kimball's staff polled the public and determined that, true to his predictions, the period rooms were the most popular part of the collection.[49]

The building proffered other important attractions, however. The hilltop temple bewitched the cast of the popular musical *Houseboat on the Styx*, who danced a May Day caper around its columns in 1929 (fig. 3-32), and that fall its innovations lured the British architect Sir Edwin Lutyens to Philadelphia. Lutyens, who was then building the city of New Delhi, capital of British India, and who could fairly claim to be the leading classical architect in the world, visited the museum on October 7, 1929 (fig. 3-33). He met with Kimball and pronounced himself impressed by the arrangements for artificial lighting and the decorative polychromy. "'It makes me jealous,'" he said.[50]

Not all reviews of the new building were positive, of course. The painter Henry McCarter, who derided the building as an anachronistic "Greek garage," felt it deserved "'no

Figure 3-33. Sir Edwin Lutyens (right), the famed English classical architect, met Fiske Kimball (left) and praised the new museum on October 7, 1929.

Figure 3-34. The medieval section welcomed the public on March 16, 1931. At its center, Kimball created a French Romanesque cloister that incorporated architectural elements from the late thirteenth-century Abbey of Saint-Genis-des-Fontaines. The twelfth-century fountain came from the Monastery of Saint-Michel-de-Cuxa.

place in a modern city.'"[51] He was especially critical of the absence of natural light in the galleries, a view shared by Harrison S. Morris, former managing director of the Pennsylvania Academy of the Fine Arts in Philadelphia, where McCarter taught. Morris also faulted the ventilation and attacked the unavoidable failure of the period room windows to align with those of the museum's masonry exterior. Most ominously, he predicted that the untested yellow limestone would crack and decay after a few years of exposure; in short, "'The museum, with its high cost, has been handed us as an inappropriate gold brick.'"[52]

Kimball was undaunted by such aspersions and continued to pursue his plans. Within a year of the opening he had acquired almost all of the historic interiors needed to line his second-floor "main street," and in 1930 the installation of these new attractions began in the south wing with the reerection of the stern French Romanesque church portal from the Augustinian Abbey of Saint-Laurent, through which one passed into a serene cloister assembled from elements of the Romanesque Abbey of Saint-Genis-des-Fontaines (fig. 3-34). These and the other medieval galleries opened to the public on March 16, 1931, after a brief ceremony at which the Gothic Revival architect Ralph Adams Cram alluded to the social unrest of the Depression and opined, rather unconvincingly, "'Today we are beginning to realize that in the medieval period there were values that we have lost that may enable us to solve problems now before us.'"[53]

Kimball oversaw the work of installing the interiors with the assistance of his own staff architect, Erling H. Pedersen, who had come to work for him in Philadelphia before the 1928 opening. Kimball also continued to collaborate with the original team of architects, among whom Charles Borie remained the partner in charge, but with the increasingly visible participation of Julian Abele, the talented African American architect from Trumbauer's office, where most of the drawings were prepared (see fig. 2-6). Abele had contributed vibrant perspectives of the design at earlier dates (see figs. 1-6, 1-13, 1-15, 1-16, 2-22, 2-23), and among his later work on the project was a set of rendered sections and plans with which Kimball illustrated his vision for the completed building in the November 1934 issue of the museum's *Bulletin*. Abele earned Kimball's respect, and in 1942 the museum director wrote in support of his membership in the American Institute of Architects, calling him "one of the most sensitive designers anywhere in America."[54]

As the Depression settled over the United States, Kimball and his team were compelled to adapt to new conditions. The museum was saddled by debt from the purchase of the Foulc Collection of important medieval and Renaissance decorative arts, former donors were

Figure 3-35. With the support of the Works Progress Administration, Kimball contrived to install most of his collection of period rooms in 1935–43. Presided over by the Hugh Ferriss rendering of the museum at left (see fig. 3-27), a large team of WPA architects produced the necessary construction drawings.

Figure 3-36. WPA craftsmen assembled the sixteenth-century English paneling from Red Lodge in 1936.

unable to continue their giving, and the city withdrew most of its support, cutting the museum appropriation from $189,000 in 1930–31 to $50,000 in 1933–34. There seemed to be little prospect now that the dozen or so remaining period interiors would soon be installed, and the museum was forced to cut the director's salary and lay off most of its paid curators, replacing them with volunteers where possible. In 1934 the museum could only afford to open to the public three and one-half days a week.[55]

The Depression did, however, reap Kimball one windfall. In mid-1933, shortly after the unveiling of the Jennewein pediment marked the end of the original construction program, the trustee of John G. Johnson's will proposed the "temporary" transfer of the paintings to the museum of art, citing the city's financial inability to maintain Johnson's former home as a gallery. Although the decision would have to be defended repeatedly in court until a definitive ruling in 1989, the Johnson Collection, some of which had already been "borrowed" for the 1928 grand opening and again when the medieval galleries were inaugurated in 1931, was never to leave the museum.[56] To display the additional paintings, Kimball rapidly fitted up galleries on the first floor of the north wing, which had originally been designated for study collections, thus undermining his own master plan. For the first time he was faced with the pleasant quandary of having too much art.

Kimball endeavored with limited success to exploit the programs of the federal Public Works Administration for the benefit of the museum, and when Congress authorized the more potent Works Progress Administration (WPA) in May 1935, he quickly designed a scheme to install his backlog of period interiors. By counting the value of the already-purchased historical materials as the museum's mandatory contribution, he was able to sponsor a series of work programs, starting with the first WPA project in Pennsylvania in November 1935 and continuing until 1943. The total federal expenditure approached $2 million.[57] Scores of architects worked in the museum drafting room during this period, drawing the construction plans needed by the installers (fig. 3-35). The installation craftsmen themselves represented almost every conceivable specialization, for reassembling the historic interiors required mastery of wood, stone, tile, plaster, iron, and glass, while their modern home was built of steel and concrete, lit by electricity, and heated by steam.

By the winter of 1936–37, various Dutch, German, French, English, and Italian rooms acquired for the north wing could be opened to the public (fig. 3-36), and the first of the major Asian interiors (the Sasanian portal, Persian tile panels, Indian temple, and Ming palace hall) were inaugurated on the building's south side in April 1940 (figs. 3-37, 3-38). The

Figures 3-37, 3-38. The hall from a Ming dynasty nobleman's palace in Beijing had been acquired by the museum in 1929, when Kimball was racing to complete his "main street" of art. The great seventeenth-century roof timbers were fitted into place by WPA workers in November 1937 (above).

Figure 3-39. The most dazzling of the museum's European period rooms, Robert Adam's drawing room from Lansdowne House in London (c. 1766–75), was purchased in 1931 and unveiled in Philadelphia in 1943. In order to match the room's windows with those in the external wall of the museum, Kimball had to rearrange some of the woodwork.

French Rococo salon from the Château de Draveil and the virtuosic Robert Adam–designed drawing room from Lansdowne House in London were installed in 1940 and 1943, respectively, thus finishing the museum's nearly complete survey of European architectural art from 1400 to 1800 (fig. 3-39).

The WPA teams also fitted out the first-floor galleries of the north wing for the Johnson Collection, and in the south wing, in part of the area now occupied by the Dorrance Special Exhibition Galleries and the American Collections, they built the first and only substantial part of Kimball's intended suite of study collections to be completed, with rooms for prints and drawings, ceramics, glass, textiles, and woodwork (fig. 3-40). In the south wing of the ground floor, where the main museum store and the Berman and Stieglitz Galleries are now, the WPA craftsmen finally constructed Kimball's much vaunted education department in 1942, equipped with classrooms and special exhibition facilities. The north wing at this level was devoted to administrative offices and the library (where they are still located) and a tea room, open to staff and the public alike.

After the war, Kimball secured the important twentieth-century collections of A. E. Gallatin and Louise and Walter Arensberg for the museum, installing the latter in 1954 in a group of galleries at the end of the first floor of the north wing. Knowing that the Arensbergs "didn't want the architecture too damn Wright-y" (in the modern manner of Frank Lloyd Wright),[58] he designed the central Arensberg room on the model of a small, basilical church (fig. 3-41). This work, which he undertook himself in consultation with the Arensbergs' friend Marcel Duchamp, was his last notable contribution to the building before retiring in January 1955.

Kimball's successor was Henri Marceau, who had arrived at the museum in 1927 as curator of the then-independent Johnson Collection and was soon hired by Kimball as

Figure 3-40 (*above*). The WPA constructed the study collections Kimball wanted on the first floor of the south wing, including these galleries for the print department (shown here in a 1952 photograph), with a mezzanine for offices above them.

Figure 3-41 (*left*). One of Kimball's greatest accomplishments was bringing the collection of Louise and Walter Arensberg to the museum. He designed a chapel-like setting for their twentieth-century and pre-Columbian art, photographed here a few months before the official opening in October 1954.

Figures 3-42, 3-43. The museum's Japanese teahouse was accorded a formal farewell ceremony in Tokyo in September 1928 (above), before being dismantled and shipped to Philadelphia. Finally installed in 1957 (right), it is the work of the early twentieth-century traditionalist architect Ōgi Rodō, who incorporated elements from an eighteenth-century building.

curator of paintings and sculpture. Like Kimball an architect by training, Marceau committed himself to the completion of Kimball's master plan, with the continuing assistance of Erling Pedersen.

Major construction projects marked almost every year of Marceau's directorship (1955–64). In 1957, the opening of the Japanese teahouse and temple (acquired in 1928 and 1929, respectively) completed Kimball's long-deferred plan for the Asian period rooms on the upper floor of the south wing (figs. 3-42, 3-43). In 1958, fifteen galleries for American decorative arts were completed on the first floor of that wing, and the Charles Patterson Van Pelt Auditorium was inaugurated in January 1959. The latter was the masterpiece of Pedersen's long association with the museum: a serene space decorated in the favored colors of the time—turquoise upholstery, apricot stage curtain, beige wall covering, and brown carpet.

Many of the major painting galleries on the first and second floors of the north wing, which had been fitted up as cheaply as possible in the 1920s and 1930s, were revisited by Marceau and Pedersen in a major campaign to improve lighting and finishes in 1959–61. The most dramatic of Marceau's projects was the refurbishing of the great stair hall in 1962–63, when a permanent ceiling was at last installed. The wooden balcony railings were not replaced with bronze until 1976.

Evan Turner took over as director upon Marceau's retirement in 1964. He championed the improvement of educational services, culminating in the conversion of much of the old entrance tunnel on the south side of the building into a student center, named on the occasion of its dedication in January 1969 for former museum president Bernice McIlhenny Wintersteen. For the first time since the original design was created by Trumbauer, Zantzinger, Borie, and Medary, the museum turned to an outside architect for this work, selecting the Philadelphia firm of Geddes, Brecher, Qualls, and Cunningham.

Figures 3-44, 3-45. In preparation for the Philadelphia celebration of the Bicentennial of the United States in 1976, the museum created a new, much larger gallery for temporary exhibitions, expanding into an unfinished area that had served as storage. The space has no permanent partitions, allowing inventive installations like those created for the *Federal Philadelphia* (left) and *Constantin Brancusi* (above) exhibitions in 1987 and 1995, respectively.

Figure 3-46. In 1977 a two-story "armory" for the Kienbusch Collection opened in the vast gallery originally intended for special exhibitions.

Growing demands for exhibition and office space prompted the consideration of radical solutions, and in 1971 the same firm sketched a westward extension of the museum in the form of an enormous terrace that reached out toward the Schuylkill River. Rejecting that plan as both too costly and intrusive, the museum sought other answers from the architects, and in 1975–76, in preparation for the expected influx of crowds during the Bicentennial celebration, they reconfigured the underutilized space on the first floor of the south wing. The study collections of ceramics, glass, and woodwork (see fig. 3-40), and three galleries devoted to a permanent display of costume, were now replaced by a chronological installation of American painting, furniture, and decorative art. The departments of costume and textiles, prints, drawings, and photographs, and other curatorial offices were moved up to mezzanines over the new American wing and expanded special exhibition galleries (figs. 3-44, 3-45). At the same time, the ground floor of the south wing was also reorganized, with the museum store, cafeteria, and education department relocated to their present positions and a new restaurant added to the amenities. Perhaps the most appreciated component of this mammoth project was the installation of a building-wide air conditioning system.

Turner hired Philadelphia's most famous architects, Robert Venturi and Denise Scott Brown, to design the Bicentennial exhibition, *Philadelphia: Three Centuries of American Art,* which inaugurated the special exhibition galleries in 1976. The next year the museum opened its new American galleries, designed by John Caulk III, and an "armory" for the Kienbusch Collection of Arms and Armor (fig. 3-46). The latter was inserted in the large gallery at the head of the great stair that had been originally intended as a special exhibition space (see fig. 1-4) but was used as an auditorium during much of the museum's early history. Curatorial offices and a new meeting room for the board of trustees were built in the mezzanine spaces around the armory's majestic hall.

In 1980, under the leadership of director Jean Sutherland Boggs, the museum again retained the services of Venturi and Scott Brown, this time to prepare a new master plan. Together with the architects, Boggs, museum president Henry P. McIlhenny, and an increasingly professionalized curatorial staff focused on the fundamental reorganization of the museum's collections. They returned for inspiration to Kimball's fifty-five-year-old vision of a single, chronologically arranged "main street" of art, which had been gradually blurred by the museum's separate display of some of the important private collections it had acquired, most notably the Johnson Collection, whose holdings spanned seven centuries of European painting. The new plan called for the integrated, chronological ordering of all major Euro-

Figure 3-47. In 1992–95, the European collections were rehung in the spirit of Fiske Kimball's "main street" of art. This axial view through the south wing shows the medieval galleries, with Rogier van der Weyden's *Crucifixion* in the distance (see fig. 1-11). The bronze and stone railings in the foreground were installed in 1976, and the superb suite of tapestries on the life of Constantine, designed by Peter Paul Rubens and Pietro da Cortona (visible to each side of the doorway), was a gift of the Kress Foundation in 1959.

pean holdings and the reestablishment of the somewhat neglected function of the period rooms as galleries for the display of paintings and other objects. There was, however, to be no attempt to create Kimball's parallel system of study collections, for which there was now little demand and no room.

Anne d'Harnoncourt, formerly curator of twentieth-century art, became director in 1982, and Robert Montgomery Scott became the museum's first professional, salaried president at the same time. Under their leadership the Venturi–Scott Brown master plan was implemented, revolutionizing the appearance of ninety of the museum's permanent collection galleries. With the endorsement of an international committee of experts, this vast project was put in motion under the architectural direction of Jeffrey D. Ryan (Jackson and Ryan, Houston), previously a member of Venturi and Scott Brown's office. In successive phases between 1992 and 1995, the galleries of European art before 1900 were entirely rehung, with paintings from all the museum's European collections assembled into a grand chronological sequence that also embraced the period rooms (fig. 3-47). Not since the time of Fiske Kimball had the Philadelphia Museum of Art offered so many new experiences.

The only major aspect of this work to betray visibly Venturi and Scott Brown's distinctive stylistic traits was the colorful redecoration of the gravely Doric west lobby, a respectful yet inventive response to the building's modernistic classicism. A vast public information desk, topped by an electric signboard and neon griffins, was installed as a centerpiece in 1988 (fig. 3-48), with a subtly modulated pastel color scheme applied to the ceiling and walls and new "classical" furniture built specifically for the museum.

The combination of idealism and pragmatism with which the Philadelphia Museum of Art has faced its recent challenges might well have pleased Fiske Kimball, who would also be glad to see that his organizational scheme was now respected as much as ever. He had forecast that "the perfect museum will never be built, still less reduced to formula," but he enjoyed the challenges of making the attempt.[59] So have those who followed him in command of Fairmount's great temple of art.

Figure 3-48. Robert Venturi and Denise Scott Brown's bold information desk was installed as part of their redecoration of the west lobby in 1988. In the adjacent stair hangs Marc Chagall's painted backdrop for Léonide Massine's 1942 ballet *Aleko*.

Figure 3-49. Fireworks bathe the museum with color in the pyrotechnic finale of Philadelphia's Fourth of July concert in 1994.

1. "Dual Art Gallery Idea Abandoned," *Public Ledger,* July 20, 1920, p. 1.

2. "Widener Quits Art Jury; City Loses Pictures," *Public Ledger,* July 23, 1920, pp. 1, 4.

3. Richard Dorment, *British Painting in the Philadelphia Museum of Art: From the Seventeenth through the Nineteenth Century* (Philadelphia, 1986), pp. xiii–xvi.

4. Charles Willis Thompson, "Park Commission and Art Jury Toploftically Refuse News of the Art Museum," *Public Ledger,* October 10, 1921, p. 2.

5. Fairmount Park Commission Minutes, vol. 14, pp. 233–35, November 22, 1922, City of Philadelphia, Department of Records, City Archives (hereinafter cited as City Archives of Philadelphia), 149.1; "Art Museum Cost Put at $8,500,000; Finished in Two Years," *Public Ledger,* November 23, 1922, pp. 1, 5.

6. "Taxpayers Quiz $8,500,000 Cost for Art Museum," *Evening Public Ledger,* January 8, 1923, pp. 1, 13.

7. "Lowest Bidders for Art Museum Building Ignored," *Evening Public Ledger,* January 9, 1923, pp. 1, 6.

8. Fairmount Park Commission Minutes, vol. 14, pp. 277–78, June 13, 1923, City Archives of Philadelphia, 149.1.

9. Fairmount Park Commission Minutes, vol. 14, pp. 316–18, April 17, 1924, City Archives of Philadelphia, 149.1.

10. Fairmount Park Commission Minutes, vol. 14, pp. 473–75, December 14, 1927, City Archives of Philadelphia, 149.1.

11. Langdon Warner to Charles Borie, September 14, 1921, and Borie to Warner, September 15, 1921; Philadelphia Museum of Art Archives, WAR (Warner Records), series 1, file "WRA—X, Y, Z."

12. See Steven Eric Bronson, "John Gregory: The Philadelphia Museum of Art Pediment" (master's thesis, University of Delaware, 1977).

13. See Shirley Reiff Howarth, *C. Paul Jennewein, Sculptor* (Tampa, 1980).

14. Leon V. Solon, "Principles of Polychrome in Sculpture Based on Greek Practice," *The Architectural Record,* vol. 43, no. 6 (June 1918), pp. 526–33.

15. David Van Zanten, "The Architectural Polychromy of the 1830s" (Ph.D. diss., Harvard University, 1970); R. D. Middleton, "Hittorff's Polychrome Campaign," in *The Beaux-Arts and Nineteenth-Century French Architecture,* ed. Robin Middleton (Cambridge, Mass., 1982), pp. 174–95; Marie-Françoise Billot, "Research in the Eighteenth and Nineteenth Centuries on Polychromy in Greek Architecture," in *Paris, Rome, Athens: Travels in Greece by French Architects in the Nineteenth and Twentieth Centuries,* by the Ecole Nationale Supérieure des Beaux-Arts, Paris; National Gallery, Athens; Museum of Fine Arts, Houston; and IBM Gallery of Science and Art, New York (Houston, 1982), pp. 61–126.

16. This account draws heavily on Leon V. Solon, "The Philadelphia Museum of Art, Fairmount Park, Philadelphia: A Revival of Polychrome Architecture and Sculpture," *The Architectural Record,* vol. 60, no. 2 (August 1926), pp. 96–111.

17. Fairmount Park Commission Minutes, vol. 13, pp. 183–84, November 9, 1921, City Archives of Philadelphia, 149.1.

18. Northeast niche: "ΕΚ ΓΑΙΗΣ ΓΑΡ ΠΑΝΤΑ ΚΑΙ ΕΙΣ ΓΗΝ ΠΑΝΤΑ ΤΕΛΕΥΤΑ" ("For all things are from the earth, and to the earth all things return," Xenophanes 21.B.27, from Hermann Diels, *Die Fragmente der Vorsokratiker,* 6th ed., ed. Walther Kranz [Berlin, 1951], vol. 1, p. 135); north tunnel portal (loading dock): "ΑΡΙΣΤΟΝ ΜΕΝ ΥΔΩΡ" ("Water is best," Pindar, *Olympia* I); southeast niche: "Η ΨΥΧΗ Η ΗΜΕΤΕΡΑ ΑΗΡ ΟΥΣΑ ΣΥΓΚΡΑΤΕΙ ΗΜΑΣ" ("Our soul, being air, holds us together," Anaximenes 13.B.2, from Diels, *Fragmente,* vol. 1, p. 95); south tunnel portal (student center):

"ΘΕΣΠΙΔΑΕΣ ΠΥΡ" ("Fire kindled by god," Homer, passim, including *Iliad* 12.177). The identification and translation of these quotations were generously undertaken by Robert Kraft, Ralph Rosen, and Ann Blair Brownlee. See also Mary Dixon Thayer, "Museum Mottoes 'Greek' to Public," *Evening Bulletin,* April 28, 1927, p. 13.

19. Solon, "Philadelphia Museum," p. 100.

20. Ibid., p. 103.

21. Fairmount Park Commission, Minutes, vol. 13, pp. 304–6, February 13, 1924, City Archives of Philadelphia, 149.1.

22. Bronson, "Gregory," pp. 35–37.

23. Solon, "The Philadelphia Museum."

24. Mary Dixon Thayer, "Art Museum, in All Its Glory, Smiles on City While Philadelphia Bows in Admiration of Beauty," *Bulletin,* October 16, 1926, p. 16.

25. Leon V. Solon, "Principles of Architectural Polychromy," pts. 1–6, *The Architectural Record,* vol. 51 (January–June 1922), pp. 1–7, 93–100, 189–96, 285–91, 377–86, 465–75.

26. Thayer, "Museum Mottoes," p. 13. Quotations in the next six paragraphs are from this article.

27. Edward Alden Jewell, "Mainly about Sculpture," *New York Times,* May 14, 1933, sec. 9, p. 8.

28. Solon, "Philadelphia Museum," p. 111.

29. Quoted in R. Sturgis Ingersoll, "The Creation of Fairmount," *Philadelphia Museum of Art Bulletin,* vol. 61, nos. 287–88 (Fall 1965–Winter 1966), p. 25.

30. George Roberts and Mary Roberts, *Triumph on Fairmount: Fiske Kimball and the Philadelphia Museum of Art* (Philadelphia, 1959); Lauren Weiss Bricker, "The Writings of Fiske Kimball: A Synthesis of Architectural History and Practice," in *The Architectural Historian in America: A Symposium in Celebration of the Fiftieth Anniversary of the Founding of the Society of Architectural Historians,* ed. Elisabeth Blair MacDougall (Washington, D.C., 1990), pp. 215–35; Bricker, "The Contributions of Fiske Kimball and Talbot Faulkner Hamlin to the Study of American Architectural History" (Ph.D. diss., University of California at Santa Barbara, 1992).

31. Klaus Streckebach, "Museumsbauten," in *Berlin und seine Bauten,* pt. 5, vol. A, *Bauten für die Kunst,* ed. Robert Riedel (Berlin, 1983), pp. 13–52; Edward P. Alexander, "Wilhelm Bode and Berlin's Museum Island: The Museum of World Art," in *Museum Masters* (Nashville, 1983), pp. 207–38; Achim Preiss, *Das Museum und seine Architektur: Wilhelm Kreis und der Museumsbau in der erste Hälfte des 20. Jahrhunderts* (Alfter, Germany, 1993), pp. 113–25.

32. Fiske Kimball, "The Museum of the Future," *Creative Art,* vol. 4, no. 4 (April 1929), p. xli. See also Kimball, "The Modern Museum of Art," *The Architectural Record,* vol. 66, no. 6 (December 1929), pp. 559–80; Kimball, "Planning the Art Museum," ibid., pp. 581–90; Erling H. Pedersen, "Outline Reminder for Museum Specifications," ibid., pp. 591–94.

33. "City's New Art Museum to Be Minus Fatigue," *Inquirer,* October 9, 1927, sec. B, p. 1.

34. Ibid., p. 2.

35. Kimball, "Museum of the Future," p. xxxvii.

36. An eighteenth-century room from Tower Hill in London and the fragments of three sixteenth-century Indian temples.

37. "City's New Art Museum to Be Minus Fatigue," p. 2.

38. Kimball, "Planning," pp. 589–90; C. E. Weitz, "The Philadelphia Museum of Art—Introduces a New Technique in the Art of Lighting Art," *Light,* May 1928, pp. 5–7, 22–23, 33.

39. Weitz, "Philadelphia Museum," p. 33.

40. Kimball, "Museum of the Future," p. xxxix.

41. "Art Museum Plans Educational Work," *Inquirer,* February 19, 1928, sec. B, p. 13.

42. "Experts Approve Phila. Art Plans," *Public Ledger,* November 6, 1927, p. 7; "$350,000 Fund Is Offered Art Museum Here," *Public Ledger,* November 29, 1927, pp. 1, 4.

43. Sarah D. Lowrie, "As One Woman Sees It," *Public Ledger,* January 8, 1928, pp. 1, 5.

44. "600 View Paintings at City Museum," *Bulletin,* March 8, 1928, p. 29; "Art Gallery's Magnificence a Revelation," *Record,* March 8, 1928, pp. 1, 4; Richard J. Beamish, "Loophole Seen to Put Johnson Art in Museum," *Inquirer,* March 8, 1928, pp. 1, 4; "600 Get First View of City's Museum," *Public Ledger,* March 8, 1928, pp. 1, 4.

45. John M. McCullough, "Preview Starts Art Museum Drive for $1,850,000," *Inquirer,* March 14, 1928, pp. 1, 7; "New Art Museum Greatly Admired by French Envoy," *Record,* March 14, 1928, p. 5; "Claudel Extols New Art Museum," *Public Ledger,* March 14, 1928, p. 5.

46. John M. McCullough, "20-Year Effort Ends in Opening of Art Museum," *Inquirer,* March 27, 1928, pp. 1, 7; Henry Hart, "6000 See 20-Year 'Dream' Realized for Art Museum," *Public Ledger,* March 27, 1928, pp. 1, 2. See also "The 'Wonderful Greek Garage,'" pages 29–43 above.

47. "Philadelphia's Splendid Museum of Art," *Inquirer,* March 27, 1928, p. 12; "The Pride of Philadelphia," *Bulletin,* March 26, 1928, p. 8.

48. "Art Museum Still Drawing Thousands," *Inquirer,* March 28, 1928, p. 2; "Near 1,000,000 Visit Phila. Art Museum during First Year," *Inquirer,* July 14, 1929, p. 1.

49. "Visitors to Art Museum Announce Preferences," *Public Ledger,* November 29, 1929, p. 2.

50. "Noted Architects Visit Art Museum," *Bulletin,* October 8, 1929, p. 23.

51. "$25,000,000 Art Museum, Ugh! Fine Greek Garage," *Record,* November 16, 1928, pp. 1, 4.

52. "Museum's Walls Expected to Peel by Art Director," *Record,* November 23, 1928, p. 3.

53. Cram quoted in Dorothy Grafly, "Thousands Drawn to Art Museum," *Public Ledger,* March 17, 1931, p. 3; see also Arthur Edwin Bye, "Glory of Medieval France Is Recreated on Parkway," *Record,* March 15, 1931, sec. B, p. 2; "Handbook of the Display Collection of the Art of the Middle Ages," *The Pennsylvania Museum Bulletin,* vol. 26, no. 140 (March 1931), pp. 2–47; "The Display Collection of the Art of the Middle Ages," *The Pennsylvania Museum Bulletin*, vol. 26, no. 141 (April 1931), pp. 2–27; and "Pennsylvania Museum Exhibition Opens," *The Art News*, vol. 29, no. 25 (March 21, 1931), pp. 3, 8, 27–35.

54. Kimball to the American Institute of Architects, April 6, 1942, Philadelphia Museum of Art Archives, FKR (Fiske Kimball Records), series 1, file "A thru B, 1942."

55. "Head of Museum Bares Fund Need," *Public Ledger,* April 12, 1934, p. 2; "Depression Keeps Priceless Art in Museum Storage," *Inquirer,* April 22, 1934, sec. E, pp. 1, 2; Weldon Bailey, "Museum Work Halted by Insufficient Funds," *Record,* April 29, 1934, sec. A, pp. 6, 9.

56. Roberts and Roberts, *Triumph on Fairmount,* pp. 130–43.

57. "Brief History of W.P.A. Construction at the Philadelphia Museum of Art, 1935–1937," November 5, 1937, Philadelphia Museum of Art Archives, FKR, series 2, sec. 4(18), file "WPA Projects at Museum, 1936–1940"; Charles J. Cummiskey, "Closing Report of Project," May 23, 1940, ibid.; "The Philadelphia Museum of Art," January 20, 1943, Philadelphia Museum of Art Archives, FKR, series 2, sec. 4(17), file "Financial Account of Projects, 1938–43."

58. Kimball to Louise and Walter Arensberg, June 7, 1951, Arensberg Collection, Department of Twentieth-Century Art, Philadelphia Museum of Art.

59. Kimball, "Modern Museum," p. 580.

Photographic Credits

Figure 1-1 Photograph by Graydon Wood

Figure 1-2 Department of Records, City Archives, City of Philadelphia, 116.01, 25260

Figure 1-3 *Evening Ledger,* March 27, 1928

Figure 1-4 Philadelphia Museum of Art Archives (hereinafter cited as PMAA), Construction Scrapbook 4, photograph 127. Photograph by William R. Hellerman

Figure 1-5 PMAA, Construction Scrapbook 4, photograph 129. Photograph by William R. Hellerman

Figure 1-6 Attributed to Julian Abele, delineator. Crayon on tracing paper, mounted on card; 16 x 18 7/8" (40.6 x 47.9 cm). PMAA, 60.1. Photograph by Andrew Harkins

Figure 1-7 *Bulletin,* March 28, 1928

Figure 1-8 "A Portfolio of Views of the New Museum Building," *The Pennsylvania Museum Bulletin,* vol. 23, no. 120 (April 1928), p. 10

Figure 1-9 PMAA

Figure 1-10 PMAA, Construction Scrapbook 4, photograph 107. Photograph by William R. Hellerman

Figures 1-11, 1-12 PMAA, Kimball Scrapbook, 1928–1930s

Figure 1-13 Attributed to Julian Abele, delineator. Crayon and graphite on tracing paper, mounted on board; 13 x 18 1/8" (33 x 46 cm). PMAA, 60.3. Photograph by Lynn Rosenthal

Figure 1-14 "The Philadelphia Museum of Art," *The Pennsylvania Museum Bulletin,* vol. 30, no. 164 (November 1934), p. 24

Figure 1-15 Attributed to Julian Abele, delineator. Crayon on cardboard, 23 3/4 x 25 3/8" (60.3 x 64.4 cm). PMAA, 60.12. Photograph by Lynn Rosenthal

Figure 1-16 Attributed to Julian Abele, delineator. Graphite and crayon on tracing paper, mounted on board; 20 x 24" (50.8 x 61 cm). PMAA, 60.9. Photograph by Lynn Rosenthal

Figure 1-17 PMAA, Construction Scrapbook 4, photograph 100. Photograph by William R. Hellerman

Figure 1-18 *Thirty-Ninth Annual Report of the City Parks Association of Philadelphia* (1927–28), p. 27

Figure 1-19 PMAA, SF/PHO, Box 1a. Photograph by Sigurd Fischer

Figure 1-20 Photograph by Graydon Wood

Figure 2-1 Gréber office, delineators. Watercolor and ink on paper, 55 3/8 x 219 3/8" (140.6 x 557.2 cm) (overall). PMAA, 90.9a (detail). Photograph by Graydon Wood

Figure 2-2 Photograph by Graydon Wood

Figure 2-3 J. Hutchinson, delineator; February 24, 1892. Photograph of lost drawing (detail). Print and Picture Collection, The Free Library of Philadelphia

Figure 2-4 Photograph of lost drawing (detail); 1895, redrawn 1900. Henry Bacon Collection, Wesleyan University Archives, Middletown, Connecticut

Figure 2-5 Print and Picture Collection, The Free Library of Philadelphia. Photograph by W. N. Jennings

Figure 2-6 James T. Maher Archives, courtesy Mrs. Helena S. Fennessy

Figure 2-7 Paul P. Cret, delineator. Lithograph, 34 x 31 3/4" (86.4 x 80.6 cm). PMAA, 90.1. Photograph by Andrew Harkins

Figure 2-8 Photograph of lost originals. Department of Records, City Archives, City of Philadelphia, 117.01, 4750

Figure 2-9 William E. Groben, delineator. Photograph of lost watercolor. Department of Records, City Archives, City of Philadelphia, 117.01, 4762

Figure 2-10 Attributed to Zantzinger, Borie, and Medary office, delineators. Photograph of lost watercolor. PMAA, SF/PHO, Box 1 (detail)

Figure 2-11 Attributed to Horace Trumbauer office, delineators. Blueline print, 11 1/2 x 26 1/2" (29.2 x 67.3 cm). PMAA, 20.4 (detail). Photograph by Graydon Wood

Figure 2-12 Attributed to Horace Trumbauer office, delineators. Watercolor and graphite on paper, 23 1/4 x 51 1/2" (59 x 130.8 cm). PMAA, 20.7 (detail). Photograph by Graydon Wood

Figure 2-13 Zantzinger, Borie, and Medary office, delineators. Graphite, ink, watercolor, and wash on illustration board; 10 1/4 x 23 3/4" (26 x 60.3 cm). PMAA, 30.7 (detail). Photograph by Laura Voight

Figure 2-14 Zantzinger, Borie, and Medary office, delineators. Graphite on illustration board, 21 7/8 x 29 7/8" (55.6 x 75.9 cm). PMAA, 30.13. Photograph by Lynn Rosenthal

Figure 2-15 William Pope Barney, delineator. Graphite, ink, crayon, and watercolor on paper; 15 x 43 1/4" (38.1 x 109.9 cm). PMAA, 40.3. Photograph by Graydon Wood

Figure 2-16 William Pope Barney, delineator. Graphite on tracing paper, 11 3/4 x 17 3/4" (29.8 x 45.1 cm). PMAA, 40.7. Photograph by Laura Voight

Figure 2-17 The Athenaeum of Philadelphia

Figure 2-18 Attributed to Howell Lewis Shay, delineator. Photograph of lost drawing. PMAA, SF/PHO, Box 1 (detail)

Figure 2-19 Attributed to Howell Lewis Shay, delineator. Photograph of lost drawing. PMAA, SF/PHO, Box 1 (detail)

Figure 2-20 From *Yearbook of the Twenty-Second Annual Architectural Exhibition Held by the Philadelphia Chapter of the American Institute of Architects and the T-Square Club* (Philadelphia, 1916)

Figure 2-21 Photograph of lost model. PMAA, SF/PHO, "PMA—Models of Proposed Museums"

Figure 2-22 Julian Abele, delineator. Ink and crayon on paper, 32 x 75" (81.3 x 190.5 cm). PMAA, 50.6 (detail). Photograph by Lynn Rosenthal

Figure 2-23 Attributed to Julian Abele, delineator. Gouache, crayon, and graphite on tracing paper, mounted on card; 25 x 51 3/4" (63.5 x 131.4 cm). PMAA, 50.7. Photograph by Lynn Rosenthal

Figure 2-24 Jacques Gréber, delineator. Ink and crayon on tracing paper, mounted on card; 26 x 34" (66 x 86.4 cm). PMAA, 50.1. Photograph by Lynn Rosenthal

Figure 2-25 Jacques Gréber, delineator. Ink and crayon on tracing paper, mounted on illustration board; 26 x 34" (66 x 86.4 cm). PMAA, 50.2 (detail). Photograph by Lynn Rosenthal

Figure 2-26 Jacques Gréber office, delineators. Watercolor and ink on paper, 32 5/16 x 82 1/4" (82.1 x 208.9 cm) (Plexiglas package). PMAA, 50.3. Photograph by Graydon Wood

Figure 2-27 Gréber office, delineators. Watercolor, gouache, and ink on paper, 68 3/4 x 138 1/4" (174.6 x 351.2 cm). PMAA, 50.4 (detail). Photograph by Graydon Wood

Figure 3-1 Photograph by Graydon Wood

Figure 3-2 Department of Records, City Archives, City of Philadelphia, 117.01, 9992

Figure 3-3 PMAA, Construction Scrapbook 1, photograph 201. Photograph by William R. Hellerman

Figure 3-4 Benoît-Edouard Loviot, *Corner of the Parthenon,* 1879–81. Watercolor and India ink on paper, 73 5/8 x 39 3/4" (187 x 101 cm). Ecole Nationale Supérieure des Beaux-Arts, Paris, 19.307

Figure 3-5 Photograph by Graydon Wood

Figure 3-6 PMAA, SF/PHO, "PMA—Models of Proposed Museums"

Figure 3-7 PMAA, SF/PHO, "PMA—Models of Proposed Museums." Photograph by Ph. B. Wallace

Figure 3-8 PMAA, SF/PHO, "PMA—Models of Proposed Museums"

Figure 3-9 PMAA, SF/PHO, "PMA—Models of Proposed Museums." Photograph by Ph. B. Wallace

Figures 3-10, 3-11 PMAA, SF/PHO, "PMA—Building: Interior Views"

Figure 3-12 PMAA, SF/PHO, Box 1A. Photograph by S. H. Gottscho

Figure 3-13 *Architectural Record,* vol. 60, no. 2 (August 1926), p. 102. Copyright 1926 by The McGraw-Hill Companies. All rights reserved. Reproduced with the permission of the publisher.

Figure 3-14 Mary Dixon Thayer, "Art Museum, in All Its Glory, Smiles on City While Philadelphia Bows in Admiration of Beauty," *Bulletin,* October 16, 1926, p. 16

Figure 3-15 PMAA, Construction Scrapbook 3, photograph 426. Photograph by William R. Hellerman

Figure 3-16 PMAA, SF/PHO, "PMA—Building: Interior Views." Photograph by Ph. B. Wallace

Figures 3-17–3-19 PMAA, SF/PHO, "PMA Building: Pediment." Photographs by The Newell Studio

Figures 3-20–3-26 Photographs by Graydon Wood

Figure 3-27 Hugh Ferriss, delineator. Crayon on paper, 19 1/2 x 34 3/4" (49.5 x 88.3 cm). PMAA, 50.30 (detail). Photograph by Graydon Wood

Figure 3-28 *Architectural Record,* vol. 66, no. 6 (December 1929), p. 583. Copyright 1929 by The McGraw-Hill Companies. All rights reserved. Reproduced with the permission of the publisher. Photograph courtesy The Athenaeum of Philadelphia

Figures 3-29–3-31 Photographs by Graydon Wood

Figure 3-32 *Daily News,* May 1, 1929

Figure 3-33 *Bulletin,* October 8, 1929. Photograph courtesy Urban Archives, Temple University, Philadelphia

Figure 3-34 Photograph by Graydon Wood

Figures 3-35, 3-36 PMAA, FKR, series 2, section 4(19), "WPA—Photographs of Construction Projects"

Figure 3-37 Photograph by Graydon Wood

Figure 3-38 *Bulletin,* November 1937. Photograph courtesy Urban Archives, Temple University, Philadelphia

Figure 3-39 Photograph by Graydon Wood

Figure 3-40 "Handbook Number," *The Philadelphia Museum Bulletin,* vol. 47, no. 233 (Spring 1952), p. 46

Figure 3-41 Department of Twentieth-Century Art, Philadelphia Museum of Art

Figure 3-42 PMAA. Photograph by Takahashi Yoshio (Soan)

Figure 3-43 Photograph by Graydon Wood

Figure 3-44 Photograph by Will Brown

Figures 3-45–3-48 Photographs by Graydon Wood

Figure 3-49 Office of the City Representative, Philadelphia

Colophon *Philadelphia Museum of Art and the Fairmount Waterworks.* Stained-glass panels, c. 1931. Designed by Herman Schuh in the office of Irwin T. Catharine; manufactured by Columbia Art Glass Company. 90 x 46 3/4" (228.6 x 118.7 cm) (each). The School District of Philadelphia. Photograph by Graydon Wood

Index of Proper Names

DESIGNED AND COMPOSED BY
INGRID CASTRO AND ALEX CASTRO, CASTRO/ARTS, BALTIMORE
PRINTED AND BOUND BY
AMILCARE PIZZI, S.P.A., MILAN